YOUTH LEAGUE
HITTING
LIKE A CHAMP

BY
TONY OLIVA

With
Jack Clary

The Athletic Institute
North Palm Beach, FL 33480

YOUTH LEAGUE HITTING
LIKE A CHAMP

This book was produced with the cooperation of the Minnesota Twins. We would like to thank the Twins for the use of their facilities and the assistance of their personnel, especially Andy MacPhail, Tom Kelly, Kirby Puckett, Tom Mee and Laurel Prieb.

Published by The Athletic Institute
200 Castlewood Drive
North Palm Beach, Florida 33408
Printed in the United States of America

Library of Congress Catalog Card Number 89-84061
ISBN 0-87670-030x

A Word From The Publisher

This Sports Publication is but one item in a comprehensive list of sports instructional aids, such as video cassettes and 16 mm films, which are made available by The Athletic Institute. This book is part of a master plan which seeks to make the benefits of athletics, physical educational and recreation available to everyone.

The Athletic Institute is a not-for-profit organization devoted to the advancement of athletics, physical education and recreation. The Institute believes that participation in athletics and recreation has benefits of inestimable value to the individual and to the community.

The nature and scope of the many Institute programs are determined by a Professional Advisory Committee, whose members are noted for their outstanding knowledge, experience and ability in the fields of athletics, physical education and recreation.

The Institute believes that through this book the reader will become a better performer, skilled in the fundamentals of this fine event. Knowledge and the practice necessary to mold knowledge into playing ability are the keys to real enjoyment in playing any game or sport.

Howard J. Bruns
President and Chief Executive Officer
The Athletic Institute

James Hotchkiss
Executive Director
The Athletic Institute

Table of Contents

Acknowledgments xi
Foreword 1
Introduction 3

I.   The Mental Approach To Hitting   7

     Play as Much as You Can   7
     Confidence Will Come   9
     Never Be Satisfied—Mentally or Physically 10
     A Master Plan 11
     Working to Get Better 18
     Get Help and Believe in It 18
     Set Your Goals 19

II. Getting Ready 23

     Conditioning the Body for Hitting 25
     Off-Season Exercise Program 30
     Pregame Mental Preparation 35
     Taking Hitting Practice 36
     Selecting a Bat 39

III. Gripping And Choking The Bat 43

     The Grip 43
     Choking Up 48
     Who Should Choke Up? 49

IV. The Stance 53

     Width of the Stance 56
     Type of Stance 58

V.   Striding Your Way To A Better Average 63

     How Long Should You Stride? 64
     Keep That Front Foot Quiet 65
     The Hips Will Follow 67
     Staying Down and Transferring the Weight 67
     One More Time 70

VI. It's All In The Hands 73

    Position of the Hands 74
    Keep Those Hands "Quiet" 76
    Keep Both Hands on the Bat 77
    The Wrist Snap 77

VII. Arms And Shoulders: Two Key Hitting Tools 81

    Use Every Inch of Your Arms 81
    Strengthen Those Arms 84
    Better Batting from the Shoulders Up 85

VIII. The Swing Is The Thing 89

    Make it S-M-O-O-T-H 96
    Don't Change Your Swing, Move Your Feet 106
    The Quick Bat 107

IX. Bunting: It Need Not Be A Lost Art 109

    It Starts with the Mind 110
    Position of the Bat 116

X.   Building A Book On The Pitcher 121

    The Book's Table of Contents 122
    Pitching Styles 123
    Construct Your Hitting Game Plan 124

XI. Think Sharply To Hit Well 129

    Beware the Pitcher's Traps 130
    "But Doctor, I Just Can't Hit a Breaking Ball...and
    He Knows It 130
    Knowing Your Limitations and Working With Them 131
    Getting Comfortable at Bat 131
    Breaking a Slump 132
    When a "Slump" Isn't a Slump 133

XII. The Game Before The Game 135

Appendix 139
About The Authors 146

YOUTH LEAGUE HITTING

LIKE A CHAMP

Acknowledgments

It is very difficult, if not impossible, for me to give my thanks to all of those individuals whose lives have touched mine and whose influence, no matter how little or how great, has motivated me to be able to present such a project as this.

However, there are many people who come to mind and to whom I must offer my thanks for their support over the years, through good times and bad.

First, to my family. To my wife, Gordette, who has been an inspirational pillar of support, both during my active career and since it has ended, both in baseball and in life. To my children, Anita, Pedro and Ricky, whom I love very much. I wish them health and success in the years ahead of them. To Pedro, who has just begun what I sincerely hope will be a long and prosperous career as a professional baseball player, I offer my congratulations and best wishes. Being a baseball player and coach, many times I was not there to help him develop, but he, nevertheless, has developed on his own and is more than capable of making his own individual impact on the game. To my son Damion, I wish him all the best in whatever he does in life.

To my parents, Anita and Pedro. My mother is not here to see this but my father is, and he was the biggest inspiration to me in the game of baseball. To Gordette's parents, Robert and Laura Dubois, two people who mean a lot to me.

To my friend Roberto Fernandez Tapanez, the individual responsible for getting me to the pro scout who signed me and launched my career as a baseball player. To my friend Del Wilber, my manager in the instructional league, who helped me significantly as a player. To Phil Howser, my friend who, as General Manager in Charlotte, helped me through some very difficult times in my life. To my friends Minnie Mendosa and Nestor Velasquez, who took care of me during those days in Charlotte.

To the many friends that I have had over the years in baseball and namely with the Minnesota Twins organization. Calvin Griffith, my friend and business associate for many years, I particularly remember looking out for me after my active career had dimmed. He was the one who gave me my chance as a hitting instructor when it was obvious my career as an active player was coming to a close. To Carl Pohlad, the current owner of the Twins, a man I greatly respect who has polished a winner in the Twin Cities. Mr. Pohlad and Andy

McPhail are responsible for bringing me back to the big leagues, this time as a hitting instructor.

To my many friends in baseball who helped me survive the many years of playing which I was privileged to enjoy. Rod Carew, my roommate, friend and one of the best hitters to ever play the game. It was a pleasure just to watch him, let alone be his friend and roommate. To Zoilo Versailles and Camilo Pascual, my friends and teammates, who took me under their wing when I was young, näive and vulnerable. To Harmon Killebrew, whose leadership and accomplishments speak for themselves. To that entire 1965 Minnesota Twins championship team, names too numerous to mention one by one. It was great. To Sam Mele, my first big league manager, whose support helped me launch a prosperous career. To Billy Martin, another manager of mine, who was a legacy of inspiration to all, including me. To my friend Julio Becquer, a good friend. And to all those whom I have played with, played against, coached or just have had the pleasure of meeting, believe me, you have all had an influence.

To John and Wanda Harper, two people whom I consider "family" in Minnesota.

To the current Minnesota Twins organization, staff and players. It has been an inspiration for me to be involved with all of you. The world championship of 1987 was one of the greatest highlights of my career and life. To all those members of that team who made it possible and all those members of the present team who will undoubtedly try again, Frank Viola, Kent Hrbeck, Gary Gaetti, Juan Berenguer, Jeff Reardon, Dan Gladden, Greg Gagne and the rest. My special thanks to Kirby Puckett, who has been a pleasure to watch develop into one the game's finest hitters and who was also a great help to me in developing this book. To my manager and friend, Tom Kelly. To the coaches with whom I've worked, Dick Such, Rick Stelmaszek, Wayne Terwilliger and Rick Renick, thank you.

To Jim Hotchkiss, John Monteleone, Jack Clary and Mike Plunkett, without whose devotion and hard work this book would not have been possible. To my friend Lou Galgano, who has been behind me for many years.

Finally, to all of you, the fans, the people. You are the final word. You are the ultimate judges. You are the pure owners of the game and all that goes with it. To all of you, thank you.

Tony Oliva
Minneapolis,
May, 1989

FOREWORD

To those who know baseball, Tony Oliva needs no introduction. A lifetime .300 hitter and three time American League batting champion, he is a future Hall of Famer.

I have known Tony for many years. As a player, he was one of the more feared and respected hitters in the entire game. When Tony came to the plate to hit...everyone took notice. After a career shortened by injuries, he undertook coaching and managing. He is one of a select group who has succeeded not only as a natural hitter, but also as an instructor of advanced hitting technique.

I have had the pleasure of working with Tony for many years in the Minnesota Twins organization. This culminated in 1987 when the Twins won the world championship.

Now, Tony finally comes before all of America and the world with this book, which sets forth his fundamental principles of batting like a champion. What follows is a testimonial in experience and instruction to one of the game's great hitters. It should be read by all of those, on any level, who wish to improve their hitting skills.

Tom Kelly

Introduction

After nearly forty years of involvement in baseball at all levels, I truly believe what Ted Williams, one of the sport's greatest hitters, once said, "Hitting a baseball is the most difficult thing to do in all of sports." Furthermore, I also believe that hitting a baseball is a true art form, and one that demands great attention to detail as well as hours and hours of hard work.

But hitting a baseball can also be great fun, particularly if you do it well. Everyone who plays the game loves to hit, even the pitchers. I've always felt this way, ever since I began playing ball in the fields near our family home in Cuba. Although I have been retired as an active player for over ten years, I still love to take some occasional hitting around my duties as batting coach for the Minnesota Twins. There is no greater feeling in sports that the solid contact from a bat striking a ball. That is one reason why major league players love to take so much batting practice. Another reason, of course, is that they also work to become good hitters.

This book was written to help young players learn some of the basic principles of hitting a baseball so that they can become good hitters, too. I have presented much of what I tell the hitters in the Twins organization and have demonstrated those principles and techniques with numerous photographs. Study our tips and photographs and you will learn the art and science of hitting.

The secret of hitting a baseball is to do it correctly, to learn and practice the fundamentals. There are many different batting styles, but in every case, as the hitter moves through the impact area, the action of the hitters' shoulders, arms and hands is remarkably similar. Good hitters also use one other skill—they use their head and think of how they can best hit the ball, safely. This is why I insist that hitters be willing to learn the strike zone, study pitchers and compile a book on them, and learn how to hit the ball to the opposite field. These are things that I had to do to become a successful major league hitter, and I am always after our Twins batters to do the same. Kirby Puckett, one of the game's great young superstars and one of the major league's great all-around hitters, is one of my prize pupils. His fundamentally sound swing is shown on these pages...

Before young players read this book, they should be willing to accept the first commandment of the game—to work hard and use all of the principles they are taught. Knowing the way to hit is not, by itself, enough. Working to perfect those principles is a necessity, and for as long as you play the game the hard work never ceases.

I have played with, and still watch, some of baseball's great hitters, and not one of them is ever satisfied with hitting .300, or slugging 30 home runs, or batting in 100 runs. It seems that the more they accomplish the harder they want to work, because they realize there still is so much to learn about the delicate art of hitting a baseball. Many afternoons I have gone to the ball park and watched hitters like Don Mattingly of the Yankees, Wade Boggs of the Red Sox, and Tony Canseco of the Oakland A's spend an hour or more before their team's batting practice begins hitting ball after ball. And these players are among the best hitters we see every day.

So if great major league hitters like these and the fine hitters on our Twins team are never satisfied despite having been successful in the big leagues, then the only message for young players still trying to succeed is to do the same thing.

Pay attention...work hard...play the game as often as you can, and you, too, will be able to hit like a champ.

I. The Mental Approach To Hitting

There are many ways to hit a baseball, and none of them are particularly easy. Willie Stargell, the Hall of Famer of the Pittsburgh Pirates, once said, "Swing the bat as hard as you can and the ball may hit it."

I batted .304 during my major league career, and it was always a great challenge when I faced any pitcher. The key to answering the challenge was as much mental agility as it was physical ability.

There are many hitters in the big leagues who could hit over .300 every season if only they put their minds to the task. Being able to hit the ball comes as much from the confidence a batter takes to the plate as it does from all of the technical points of hitting.

From the earliest times playing baseball as a kid in Cuba until my final season in the big leagues in the mid-seventies, I never lacked for confidence, regardless of who the pitcher was. It was an attitude that I built through constant practice and playing, and with all of that work, I gained the confidence I needed to believe I could hit any pitcher I faced.

There were other spin-offs as well, such as a strong concentration level that every hitter must have to be successful, and, of course, I developed the proper techniques for following the ball and swinging the bat. People who watch the game only see the physical side...the pitcher throws, the batter swings, and the batter either hits the ball safely or he doesn't.

What few ever see, and probably fewer still even realize, is that there is a great deal of mental preparation that goes into hitting. The first key is developing the right attitude toward playing this game. Now, when I talk about playing, I mean just that—playing. Baseball is a game. It's play, and play can and should be fun. I have never understood athletes who claim to be baseball players and who look upon the game as work.

Play As Much As You Can

Thus, my first bit of advice is to play baseball...and play it as much and as often as you can. You don't have to be in an organized league to play. Heck, that is part of the problem. A lot of young players believe they must wait until the coach calls practice or until there is a game scheduled before they can play. This is not nearly enough. Play whenever you can.

When I was a youngster in Cuba, I played with adults far older than myself. In fact, a pitcher on our town team was forty years old, and I was just fifteen. But it didn't make any difference. I looked forward to every Sunday when we had a game scheduled, because it matched town against town, and it meant a lot for a player's team to win a game. I was a tall, skinny kid then, and my father took me to all the games because he knew that I could only improve my skills with experience.

"Take care of him," he told the other players when he turned me loose. "He's only fifteen so don't try to hit him."

But that was just a father trying to protect his young son from harm, which was only natural. He knew I could take care of myself on the field and at bat, because even at age fifteen I was a very good hitter. All he wanted me to do was to get as much experience as possible to become better.

Getting better is one of the key points, and you can get better only by playing, not by sitting around, talking about it, or watching other people. I have two sons who play baseball, and they were just like other kids who find all sorts of other things to do. That is why I always urged them to get together with four or five friends, to find a field, and to play baseball.

"You don't need a catcher or bases or umpires," I told them. "Play slow pitch so that everyone can hit, because the more you hit, the better you become. And you don't have to have a regulation baseball. Use a rubber ball or a tennis ball, but use something that you can hit."

And that is the same advice I give to other kids. In Cuba, if we didn't have a ball to play with, we'd scrounge around and perhaps come up with a bottle cap. It was round and we could throw it and hit it. If you can hit something as small as a bottle cap, think what you could do to a baseball. It was just another way of improving our skills. We threw those caps hard, and you can believe how hard they were to hit.

Sometimes on the way to play a game, I'd tell my brother, "I'll give you a nickel if you can strike me out today." That may not sound like much to kids today, but in Cuba in the fifties, it was a lot of money. So you know how hard I bore down to keep from striking out and how hard my brother tried to strike me out so he could get that precious nickel. It helped to make me a better hitter.

Confidence Will Come

It also helped to build my confidence level. I have played with great hitters in the big leagues who were successful because they truly believed that every time they went to the plate, regardless of who was pitching, they would be successful. Obviously, they were not, but it is a fact of baseball life that if a hitter is successful only thirty percent of the time, he is a fine hitter.

I once had a teammate in Minnesota named Cesar Tovar who came to the park every day and asked who the opposing pitcher was. It didn't matter what name he heard, he would just smile and say, "Fine. I'll get a couple of hits off him today."

I admit I was the same way. When we played the Baltimore Orioles and Jim Palmer was scheduled to pitch, it never really bothered me, even though Palmer was one of the best pitchers in the American League. I always knew how to hit against him—not to challenge his fast ball but to move my feet in the batter's box and adjust my swing so that I could hit to the opposite field. And I was very successful against Palmer. I had figured out a proper mental approach to use against one of the most overpowering pitchers of this era.

Now, don't get me wrong. I didn't just decide how I could do that and then go out and get a couple of hits. No good hitter, no matter how good his instinct may be, ever does that. My teammate Rod Carew, who was one of baseball's most consistent and successful hitters during the seventies and early eighties, was a natural hitter. But he developed himself to be a great hitter only by spending so much time in the batting cage working on his bunting, hitting balls to the opposite field, or improving his ability to pull the ball.

What does this do? Well, one season Carew got nearly three dozen hits by bunting. Just think what those bunt hits did for his average, and think, too, what his average might have been had he not achieved them. But Rod always had the attitude that he had to prove himself every time he went to bat, and he worked hard away from the game to make certain that he would be prepared to make those at bats mean something.

Tovar was another hitter like that, and today, Wade Boggs of the Red Sox and Don Mattingly of the Yankees are cut from the same mold. Tovar always had the attitude that he was better than the pitcher, even though he may have gone hitless in four at bats. I felt the same way many times, but Cesar was even able to rise above the 0-4 and convince himself that he still was better than that pitcher.

Now, he was unusual—and Ted Williams, the great left-handed slugger who played for the Red Sox in the forties and fifties and who now is in the Hall of Fame with his .344 lifetime batting average, was another—because he never gave any credit to the pitchers. But you as a batter have to be realistic—though you certainly never have to give in—and acknowledge that the pitcher is working just as hard to get you out as you are to get a hit. If he is successful, then you fail; if you are successful, then you have won the battle. There are times when it's not so simple, and you have stung the ball only to see it fly into the hands of a fielder and count as an out. But there will be other times when you will hit the baseball the same way and watch it land for a hit. The message: never give in, never give up.

Kirby Puckett, the Twins' great center fielder, is a perfect example of a player who never gives in, never gives up...and, most importantly, never stops working even though he has become an established big league star. He has a great attitude about playing the game, and he backs that up with excellent work habits. He is never satisfied with what he has achieved, even when he gets more than 200 hits a season, and he always feels he can do better. When he is hitting .340 or .320, he still comes to me and asks for extra hitting.

Never Be Satisfied—Mentally or Physically

What all of this means is that if you wish to succeed in baseball, you must be prepared to give it a full shot, to be willing to work to get better and better and to never be completely satisfied with a single performance, at least not to the point where you feel you no longer need work to improve.

While this part is physical, you must also develop the mental part of the game—be willing to take the time and apply yourself totally to whatever it takes to become a good player. Some days that may mean a couple of hours of hitting until you feel satisfied that you have begun to accomplish something. Many young players go in and take eight or nine swings and think, "Great, I've got that down. Let's go do something else."

Nothing could be further from the truth. As a hitting coach, I simply don't believe in bringing a player to the park and giving him five minutes of hitting to clear up a problem or establish his rhythm. I've always told the players that if they need extra hitting, then they must come and work until they feel comfortable. Of course, there are times when a "tune up" may do it, but that still should be twenty or thirty minutes. I just wish all the young players could see how Puckett works when he needs help, because he is just a slave to improving every facet of his hitting. If you didn't know just how great he is, you'd believe that he couldn't hit a ball.

Just to show how much that work has paid off, few may realize that Kirby used to find it easier to hit the ball to the opposite field than to pull it. Yet, with his power, he had to master pulling the ball, and he worked and worked until today he is equally adept at both skills. Hence a pitcher cannot comfortably feel that he can get him out with any single kind of pitching.

When I talk to young players at batting clinics about Kirby, the first question I get is, "How did he do it?"

"Simple," I reply, "it was hard work, even when he was hitting .290 or .300, which certainly is good enough for anyone to stay in the big leagues."

These young people look astounded when I tell them that a guy who flirts with a .300 average isn't satisfied, but I am quick to point out that Kirby always had the power to hit twenty or more home runs a year, but to do so he had to learn to pull the ball. He also had to learn the strengths and weaknesses of each pitcher, because there will be days when Roger Clemens of the Red Sox simply isn't going to allow him to pull his 95-miles-per-hour fastball into the seats for a homer. On these days, he must be content to take that fastball and drive it into the opposite field for a hit—unless, of course, Clemens should make a mistake.

Now, if he faces a pitcher whose fastball is in the low eighties, Kirby can set himself up to pull it if he gets the right pitch. To Kirby's credit, it took a lot of work and mental toughness to master those skills.

A Master Plan

This comes under the category of self-discipline, and I know that may scare some young players who look upon those words as a form of drudgery, taking the fun out of the sport. On the contrary, self-discipline in baseball is meant to do just the opposite—to make playing fun because it will help make you a better hitter. Here are some of the points which you must master:

1. Learn the strike zone. Many players say it is important to swing only at good pitches, but not everyone has good enough eyesight to swing only at strikes. Therefore, you must be ready and willing to swing at anything close to the strike zone. Remember, the only reason you swing a bat is because you think the pitch will be a strike; otherwise you'd let it go for a ball.

2. Learn to use the entire field. Later in the book we'll get more specific about how best to do this, but for now, begin to think that the

STRIKE ZONE: *Hitters must be able to cover the plate so they can go after the low strike, photo 1-1A; the "Wheelhouse" Strike in the middle of the plate, photo 1-1B; and the high strike, photo 1-1C.*

entire field belongs to your, not just right field for left-handed hitters or left field for righties.

3. Keep your eyes on the ball. It takes discipline to follow the ball from the instant it leaves the pitcher's hands until you either swing at it or it hits the catcher's glove. Don't look away or get lazy with your concentration. Remeber, the only way you can hit the ball is by seeing it. Take your eyes off it even for an instant, and you have lost that advantage.

How can you do this? First, you must establish a schedule or a regular practice routine. I mentioned before that playing baseball in any form—practice, in a game, or just with friends—should be enjoyable and a way in which you can become a better player. It means, too, not sliding away to watch videos or listen to the stereo or visit friends and hang out when you should be working at the game. I know this is tough for young players who see friends doing other things in their free time, but they probably are not too concerned with becoming good baseball players. You are concerned; therefore you must make those sacrifices.

While those of you who play for organized teams might say, "Well, we play a couple of times a week," it still means there are four or five days a week when you don't play. Those are the days when you should be out improving your skills. The most distressing sight to me is the lovely baseball fields in neighborhoods where not a single person is using them. In America, towns and cities provide such marvelous facilities, and yet they seem to go to waste.

In Latin America, where so many excellent major league players are developed, kids play on any patch of ground they can find. Some are rutted, some are pocked with holes or strewn with rocks, and some have high grass. But it doesn't matter. Kids go out and play, and they learn how to hit and field under those kinds of tough conditions. Maybe that is why so many big league shortstops—a position where you have to be adaptable, tough, and fearless—come from the Dominican Republic. The manicured diamonds you find in the United States are billiard tables compared to most of the fields down there.

I think my own kids found out about that when I took our family back to Cuba a couple of years ago to visit our relatives. We were hardly settled in when our boys' cousins came calling and wanted to play baseball. My kids didn't see any fields close by and were a bit reluctant to play, but I shooed them off because I knew those other kids had a cow pasture or meadow suitable for a game. They stayed out there for about four hours playing, and our kids came home dirty and sweaty but admitting they had a lot of fun, more fun, they said, than playing in an organized game back in Minnesota.

TAKING A PITCH: *Here Kirby shows how you must concentrate just as hard when you decide not to swing. The key to his successful taking of this pitch is keeping his front foot closed—thus keeping his hips closed and weight and hands back, always ready to launch the bat if the pitch is to be swung at— and his eyes on the ball throughout. Photos 1-2A through 1-2G show a movement that is identical to one that will result in a swing. Kirby has moved slightly down, almost squatting to follow the ball, but still undecided as to whether he will swing or not.*

TO SWING OR NOT TO SWING:
Photos 1-2H through 1-2N show what occurs when the decision not to swing has finally been made. Kirby's head and eyes follow the ball into the hitting area (photos 1-2K through 1-2N as it passes below the knee (photo 1-2M) for a called ball. Kirby will now simply "reload" and wait for a pitch he can drive.

Working To Get Better

Major league players do the same thing during the season by using their time before a game and on days when no game is scheduled. Puckett is always at the park, and so is Gary Gaetti of the Twins. When we go on the road, I may go out to the ballpark at about three in the afternoon before a night game, and if we're in New York, I'll find Don Mattingly taking extra hitting and fielding; if we're at Fenway Park in Boston, Wade Boggs is taking grounders by the dozen at third base and then going to the plate to get extra hitting long before his teammates arrive. One day in New York, I found Mattingly working with Lou Piniella and Willie Horton at Yankee Stadium.

"Are you having a problem?" I asked Don, because I knew he was hitting over .300 at the time.

He told me he needed extra work to get his timing and his swing in order, and I watched him work for nearly an hour. But a month later, I also noticed that his average had increased by thirty points.

When Carew and I played for the Twins, both of us were usually well over .300. Yet we were at the park early every day for extra hitting, not necessarily because we were having serious problems right then, but perhaps we had detected a flaw in our hitting style. In short, neither of us ever was satisfied or believed we had perfected the art of hitting a baseball.

Let me give you one more example. In 1988, Jose Canseco of the Oakland Athletics led the major leagues with forty two home runs (he also stole forty bases to become the first player in major league history ever to reach the 40–40 mark), but he is just getting better and better as a hitter. What impressed me was the fact that with all of the good numbers he was putting up during that season, he never seemed to be satisfied. In fact, he always seemed downright unhappy with the job he was doing. I used to watch him change his stance and work at different hitting styles, always trying to come up with the perfect approach. I can predict that for as long as he plays major league baseball, he will never be satisfied with his performances and will constantly work to be better. Because of that, some day he will enter the Hall of Fame.

Get Help—Believe In It

As I talk about how these great players work at the game, keep in mind that they don't do it alone, that they need and ask for help. That is the job of the team's batting coach, and part of my duties with the

Minnesota Twins. It is the same at every level of play where dedicated coaches think only of helping young players get better. Thus, it is up to the players not to turn off a coach's attempts to help them. Remember, these coaches usually know much more than the young player about hitting, and at some levels, they are really experts at the craft because they have watched hours of films and have made extensive studies of the proper way to hit a baseball.

Thus, students must pay attention to the following tips:

1. Keep an open mind and believe in the coach. If that is impossible or you simply disagree with the style he is teaching, then be honest and tell him that you would rather get instruction from someone else.

2. Players can't jump from teacher to teacher, because no teacher is going to come up with an instant magic formula to make a hitter successful. He can only show the hitter how to improve himself; it is then up to the player to take it from there and work on what he is taught. As the player progresses, his teacher always will be there to correct his flaws and to keep him on the right track. And at all times, the hitter should pay attention to him.

3. Never use the excuse of being "too tired" to work for improvement. You must come to the field every day and be willing to hit and hit and then hit some more. But don't think it will happen all at once. It probably won't even happen if you play the game for fifty years, because there hasn't been one hitter ever who really has mastered the art.

And, finally, here's a tip for the teacher. Keep it simple when instructing. You cannot be too technical because there is not much time for the hitter to think about a lot of technical details when the ball is flying at him. He should have only one thought at this time: Hit the ball.

Set Your Goals

That brings me to one last point—setting goals. Everyone, regardless of what they do in their life, must have a set of achievable goals in order to be successful. When I began playing baseball in the big leagues, mine was to be a better right fielder because I was already a fine hitter. I watched players like Al Kaline of Detroit, Roberto Clemente of the Pirates and Willie Mays of the Giants—all in the Hall of Fame today—and decided I could pattern myself after them.

"I have a good arm, I run well and I get a good jump on the ball," I told myself when I set the goal to become a good right fielder.

"Therefore, there is no reason why I can't put all of those skills together and reach that goal. If I work hard, then perhaps I'll become another Al Kaline."

And I believe I did just that. So I see nothing wrong with young players modeling themselves after great players and saying, "I can be like them." Not every player has the exact same skills, but there are certain things that great players do—I'm talking mainly about their work habits and their mental approach to the game—that everyone can follow. After that, a player's individual skills will take over and he can become as good as his talents will allow.

One thing you must remember about playing baseball: One good play will rub off to help a player make another because of the great feeling of self-confidence and achievement that it can produce. Whenever I threw out a runner on the basepaths, I came to bat feeling so good that there was little doubt in my mind that I could get a hit. And so often I did.

That is why hitting a baseball is as much a matter of mental agility as it is of physical ability.

II. Getting Ready

Long before a hitter steps to the plate, he should undergo an extensive period of self-preparation. I realize this isn't the most popular or most fun—boring, I hear some kids say—but I cannot underscore enough just how important it is if a hitter wishes to be successful. It is simply impossible to walk into the park, pick up a bat, go to the plate, and expect to get hits game after game without doing some work beforehand.

Young players who watch major leaguers see only that one side of the game. But what they miss are long hours in the off-season, in spring training and even during the season when many hitters put in as much time away from the game as they do when they play. This off-the-field preparation probably is more common now than ever before because extensive studies of athletic performances have proven that the more athletes condition themselves to play their sport, the better they will perform. In a word, everyone's doing it...or they should be.

Why is it so necessary?

Like the engine of a car that runs better after a warmup, the body of an athlete performs the same way. When I was a kid in Cuba, I got some of the best advice of my life from George Cambria, who had spent nearly ten years with the Washington Senators organization. "Tony," he said, "before you step to the plate and pick up a bat, this is what you should do..."

And he outlined a program that I followed every day of my professional life:

1. Run six or seven laps around the outfield to get loose.

2. Stretch the arms and legs to prevent muscle pulls. When your body finally loosens up after a night of inactivity, things feel good. There were times when I got to the park and was dead tired, but after doing my running and stretching, I was ready to go.

3. Soft toss a ball six or seven times before even attempting to throw it hard. This is so important because there are too many tragic stories of ruined arms of players who picked up a ball and started to fire it. Even after doing the soft lobs, stop for a couple of minutes to allow your arm and the rest of your body to get a rhythm.

GAME DAY ROUTINE: *Like a good car, your body must be warm to perform at its full capacity. Start by running in the outfield as in photo 2-1 and after your muscles are warm begin the stretching routine with the arm circles in photo 2-2. Do all of these warmup exercises eight to ten repetitions.*

2-2

GAME DAY ROUTINE; *Continue your exercises with side trunk bends to either side as in photos 2-3A and 2-3B. Be sure to bend your upper body to at least a 45-degree angle during your repetitions.*

4. After that, begin to toss the ball again, starting at 100 feet, then 120 feet, then 140, and increase the velocity of your throws to the point where you are doing it as you would in a game.

An here's a tip for thirteen- and fourteen-year-old players: Throw a lot of long tosses to help build up your arm strength—but again, only after you have warmed up beforehand.

Conditioning the Body for Hitting

I am constantly asked about conditioning programs to help improve hitting performances. There has been such a surge in conditioning and fitness awareness in this country over the past decade that all young athletes are very aware of the many methods, mostly those involving weightlifting.

Now, depending upon the sport, weightlifting must be handled in various ways. In football, where building for size and strength is so important, young athletes pump a lot of iron to get ready to play. But

GAME DAY ROUTINE: *Now start to loosen your achilles tendons by stretching them gradually and slowly, as in photo 2-4. Be certain to keep the heel of your rear foot firmly planted when doing this exercise. Alternate each leg. Stretch your back as in photo 2-5; with legs apart, bend forward slowly until you can place the bat on the top of your toes.*

2-5

GAME DAY ROUTINE: *Now we'll work on the ground, first with the Cobra Stretch shown in photo 2-6. Lay flat on the ground, place your hands outside your body frame and slowly raise your upper body until your arms are fully extended. Next flip over and stretch your quadriceps as in photo 2-7 by tucking a leg behind you and grasping it with your hand and leaning backward. You should feel a gentle tug along the top of your upper leg.*

GAME DAY ROUTINE: *Our last on-the-ground exercise is the Single Leg Hamstring Stretch shown in photo 2-8A. After tucking one leg behind you, extend the second and bend forward to grasp your foot. Now stand up and begin to stretch your throwing arm with some soft toss lobs, as in photo 2-8B. After starting at 60 to 70 feet, gradually extend the distance and velocity of your throws.*

2-8B

in baseball, where overall strength and size is not a prerequisite, I advise a different tack—one of moderation and targeting weight or resistance programs to those areas of the body that are vital for playing the game.

Don't get me wrong. I don't advocate allowing the rest of your body to be soft or not used to vigorous exercise. When I was a youngster in Cuba, I worked on a farm from the time I was in grammar school, so my body always was firm and in good shape. This is important. But as I progressed into professional baseball, I solicited help from other veterans and from trainers, and it became apparent that I needed to maintain a program of light weightlifting—curling some small barbells—to help develop my shoulders, arms, and wrists. Don't wait until you are in an advanced league to do this. Youngsters can do it simply by taking a couple of cans from their mom's pantry, holding them in their hands as they rest on a table or on their thighs, and raise and lower their arms. At the same time, roll the wrists as you lift to give them added strength. Do this for three repetitions of ten lifts, and do it every day if possible. When you get older, you can purchase the small barbells weighing ten to fifteen pounds and continue the program for as long as you play baseball.

Since baseball players need flexibility in their upper body instead of the great strength utilized by football players, they should avoid weightlifting programs that make the upper body too tight and restrict the smooth flow needed to swing the bat. Don't be misled by people in fitness centers who claim that one exercise program is good for every sport. Don't listen to friends or others who are not acquainted with the very special ways that baseball players can utilize strength programs. Instead, go to your coach, or seek help from someone who can tailor a specific program that will benefit your lower body, and add just enough work to give you the necessary strength in the upper body without binding you and causing a loss of that needed flexibility.

In the winter, use a rubber ball or a hand squeezer to build up your hand strength. Do this every day for a half hour—and you can do it while sitting in front of the TV, riding in a car, or walking down the street, so there is no excuse not to do it every day. Also work on strengthening your knees and legs in the off-season. Hitters need strong legs as much as they need strong wrists; weak legs mean a weakened body. There are weight programs available that can strengthen your lower body without tightening the upper part of your body. I believe in this type of vigorous conditioning. It will strengthen your Achilles tendons, help to prevent muscle pulls, and give you a sound base from which to swing the bat. Strong legs also mean less fatigue during the season, so that you can run the bases and field your position without slowing down.

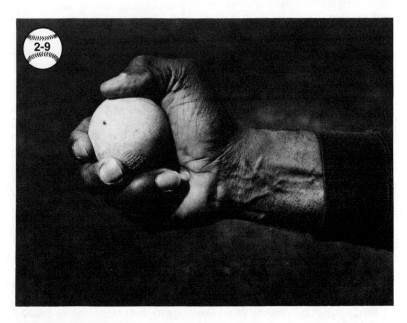

PLAY SQUEEZE BALL. *Build up your strength by squeezing a rubber ball or a hand squeezer for a half hour each day as shown in photo 2-9.*

Off-season activity is important for keeping off extra weight. You should report to spring practice in shape so that you can use the early and preseason training time for sharpening baseball skills. Your year-round program should include situps, toe touches, hamstring stretches, leg lifts, pushups, and running; in the off-season, you should work out no fewer than three times a week.

Off-Season Exercise Program

Here is a basic program that you can do in your home or nearby gym:

Activity	Frequency
1—Running.	4 times per week, 15 minutes a day
2—Bent-Knee Situps	4 times per week, 4 sets of 10 per day
3—Toe Raises	4 times per week, 3 sets of 10 per day
4—Side Twisters	4 times per week, 5 sets of 10 per day

5—Alternate Toe Touches 4 times per week, 2 sets of 25 per day

6—Pushups (Fingertip)...4 times per week, 2 sets of 10 per day

Another exercise involves rolling a weight onto a broomstick. Fasten a 15-pound weight to the end of a rope and tie the other end of the rope to the center of a 15-inch broomstick. Extend your arms to the front parallel to the ground and slowly roll the weight up and down, winding the rope around the broomstick as you rotate your wrists. Begin this exercise in December with three sets of five repetitions and work up to three sets of twenty-five repetitions just prior to preseason training. You should time this program to begin ten weeks prior to the start of your baseball team's official practices.

You may wonder what we do in the major leagues and the answer is that every player seems to have a different program. During the season, Kirby Puckett of the Twins doesn't do much with weights, but he works out extensively in the off-season to not only maintain his strength but also increase it as he gets older.

We have a couple of players on the Twins who are in our gym—we have a marvelous facility in our clubhouse with all of the necessary machines and weights needed for everyone's conditioning—every day during the season. Our trainer, Dick Martin, is the man to whom we turn for advice, and he monitors very closely the program of each player, always being careful to prescribe only what will improve that player's baseball skills.

But Dick and the rest of us all preach about one big no-no—do not ever, under any circumstances, use steroids. First of all, it has been proven that too much steroidal use can cause horrible consequences, including death, in later years. That is reason enough to steer clear, but for those who don't think it could ever happen to them, let me add that steroids will not help your baseball performance. Anything bad for your body will be bad for baseball, and only foolish people resort to this.

I know that young athletes who frequent health clubs and fitness centers get caught up in all the talk about building the perfect body, and inevitably, someone comes up with the plan to inject steroids as a quick way to produce muscle mass and strength. Forget it. Baseball players are not weightlifters and never should be. You can achieve all of the strength and muscle tone you need through a prescribed workout program that builds you naturally and safely. If anyone suggests steroids, walk away and pay no attention. They are steering you down a horrible path that can have only a tragic ending.

I'd like to make one last point: Do your conditioning program with the correct attitude. Make it a part of your weekly routine, spreading it

OFF SEASON TRAINING: *You can't wait until the first day of practice in the spring to get into shape to play. During the off-season establish a set routine that includes work on your legs, beginning with running as in photo 2-10 and bent knee situps, photo 2-11 Add some toe raises as shown in photo 2-12.*

OFF SEASON TRAINING: *The side twister shown in photos 2-13A, 2-13B, 2-13C will help to keep that waist line trim and also give your body a flexible feeling for the time when you begin to swing a bat.*

OFF SEASON TRAINING: *Work on that middle and your legs with a series of alternative toe touches as in photo 2-14, reaching to touch one foot with the opposite hand, and then reversing the procedure. Then drop down and do some fingertip push ups, shown in photo 2-15.*

out so as not to hurt yourself but yet doing it frequently enough to be effective. This is part of the self-discipline to which I referred in the preceding chapter, and it means designating specific times and days to carry it out. You must be willing to put aside other nonessential activities or other distractions and gear yourself to doing these programs. Remember, they are just as important to your career as all of the batting and fielding drills, and without them, those other facets of the game will suffer.

Pregame Mental Preparation

Before you ever get to the park, your mind should already be in the game. Hitters should be thinking about the pitcher they will face; pitchers certainly should be concentrating on the hitters who will oppose them.

What a player does before a game often determines how well he will do during the game. The first thing is to come to the park early, relax, go through your pregame exercise and begin to get pumped up and excited to play. That will happen by just being there and seeing the other team.

I'll discuss some of the pregame physical activities later in this chapter, but they really follow the necessity to get your mind ready. A hitter should be getting all the available information possible on the opposing pitcher—what he throws best and, of course, what his weaknesses are. Often the best way to be certain is to watch him yourself. Instead of kibbitzing around the bench with your teammates or friends in the stands, watch that pitcher warm up. See if he throws his fastball overhand or three-quarter sidearm or sidearm. Watch how he throws his curveball—three-quarters, sidearm, or a sinker ball effect with an overhand motion. Get a good idea of just what the ball does when it breaks. It doesn't take a major league veteran to realize that if the pitcher has a blazing fastball in his warmups, you can expect to see it about ninety percent of the time; if he concentrates on throwing good breaking pitches, then you'll see lots of them.

In the major leagues, some hitters keep a "book" on various pitchers, just as pitchers do for hitters. They will note what the pitcher throws in various situations and whether the speed, location, and selection of pitches vary with each appearance. This is a great idea, but you do not necessarily need a book. I always found that I could keep a good account in my head. Once a batter faces a pitcher for the first time, he gets a good idea of exactly what his strengths and weaknesses are—particularly if there is great success, or dismal failure.

But it is up to the player at every level to pay attention to the pitcher and be aware of what he throws. I consider it irresponsible if a player is always running to his coach and manager asking about a pitcher he already has faced several times. This means his mind is not into the game. Young players, particularly, should develop this habit from the time they start playing and keep their eyes on the pitches even while sitting on the bench.

To cite an example or two, when I was playing for the Twins, I knew that if Whitey Ford, a great left-hander, pitched for the Yankees, I was going to see a lot of screwballs. So as a left-handed batter, I knew I had to get on top of the plate to get to those nasty pitches. When Sam McDowell, another lefty, was pitching for Cleveland, I knew that I would get some tough curveballs and a fastball that rode in on me, so I prepared for those pitches. With Jim Palmer, I knew I would be going to the opposite field with his great fastball, but I also knew that I could handle it in that manner and might get a couple of hits that day.

I love the reaction of younger players when I tell them that baseball is not too different from schoolwork because both require a lot of intense study and concentration to get passing grades. A passing grade for a hitter can be going 2-for-4 or driving in the winning run, because he has studied the pitcher well enough to know what he will do in certain situations.

Another way to make this happen is by visualizing. You can do this long before you get to the park, and it is a good way to get your mind into the game. Set up certain situations—for example, men on first and second with no outs or men on second and third with two outs— and how the pitcher you will face is apt to pitch to them. Picture in your mind where you will stand in the batter's box and how that ball will look coming at your bat. Can you hit it to the opposite field? If not, can you adjust so that you can punch the ball and then visualize yourself in that position? In short, run through an imaginary game with as many different kinds of situations as possible where you as a hitter—and yes, as a fielder, too—are involved.

For instance, if you are a right-handed hitter, picture yourself moving up against a left-handed pitcher because all the pitches will be away from you. Hence, you should see yourself hitting those pitches between first and second base. Take it a step further. What if the pitcher comes inside? Then what will you do? Picture yourself moving back from the plate so you have an opportunity to get a good inside-out swing.

Taking Hitting Practice

Now comes the fun part. As I noted in the preceding chapter, the only way to become a good hitter is to hit as often as possible. Don't wait for a game or for an organized practice, but just go out with some friends and hit with anything that passes for a ball. I played with a lot of guys who as kids did this, and they used to laugh and tell how they'd knock the cover off the ball and then send someone to find some black friction tape to wrap around the ball so they could continue playing. In those discussions, they would also marvel how great it was to be in the major leagues where there was an unlimited supply of new baseballs for hitting drills.

And those players, just as the current Twins do, took advantage of that unending baseball supply. They understood that it was so necessary to get as much hitting practice as possible, and there were times when we'd have to order some of them to stop.

I like to see that same intensity in young players as well, and you don't need an endless supply of baseballs to have it. Batting practice cannot be taken lightly, and every hitter must have a set of procedures to follow to get the most from it. Here are my suggestions:

1. Be loose, and we've already discussed how to do that.
2. Be determined to make every swing mean something, especially if you are away from home and don't have a lot of time. In the majors, we only get forty minutes before a game, though we sometimes will go out early for special hitting.
3. When it's your turn to hit, have a plan. If you just punch the ball, then you miss all the good that comes from a hitting drill. Consider this routine:

(a) Bunt the first couple of pitches, not lackadaisically but as if you were in a game situation.

(b) Hit a ball as if you were given the hit-and-run sign, taking care to hit it on the ground and behind an imaginary runner. Again, be serious as if this were in the game.

(c) Hit three or four balls hard to right field if you are a lefty swinger, to left field if you are right-handed. Then hit two or three to the opposite field.

4. Above all, be serious. I know I get disturbed when I see players fooling around during batting practice because this is the most important part of their pregame work period.

It also is helpful—and it certainly makes sense—to match your batting practice pitcher with the opposition's starter. If I was to face a left-handed breaking ball pitcher, then I always wanted a lefty pitching to me in batting practice, and I wanted him to throw me some braking balls just so I could get familiar with the ball's rotation and its breaking action. Certainly, our BP man wasn't going to be as good as the opposition's pitcher, but at least I got a good idea of what the ball would do, and I was able to look at the arm motion of the pitcher and how the ball came out of his hand. These are little things, but in a game, the little things make a difference, particularly when the game is on the line and your team needs a hit.

Another point is hitting against live pitching or against a machine in practice. I always preferred a real, live batting practice pitcher, though in spring training, there are so many players it is necessary to rely on machines to get in some hitting. I know, too, that on town levels there simply aren't enough people to throw live batting practice—there aren't even enough in the minor leagues where players need as much hitting as possible—so young players must utilize machines. The machines, biggest asset really is keeping hands and arms strong, but they are not consistent in delivering pitches. As I have noted before, young players should utilize each other for batting drills and not rely simply on established practice times. A player's buddies can give him the pitches he wants, where he wants them, and with proper frequency, so the biggest asset is building the proper timing.

Proper timing also comes from frequency of practice. It is a bit silly to hit on Monday and then not pick up a bat again until Friday or the following week and expect that all you accomplished on that first day will still be in place. Hitting, above all else, demands frequent repetition, and again, young people can do that as a group any time they wish. Hey, even use a batting machine if you wish, but hit, hit, hit.

A suggestion for those who might be looking for something different: Play rotation, a game which places one player at bat, one to pitch to him, and as many positions covered in the field as there are players. A batter continues to hit until he gets out, though he never need leave the batting box. A grounder handled cleanly is an out, and the batter then goes to the farthest fielding position (usually right field) and everyone moves around one position. A fly ball or line drive to a fielder immediately brings that fielder to the plate, and the batter goes to his position. I believe you can see that with an activity such as this players get both hitting and fielding practice, in addition to having a lot of fun, and they can do it on their own terms and without an adult looking over their shoulder.

Also in this regard, when adult coaches do conduct practices, they should be careful to have all players working. Put one man at the plate, another ready to hit, and everyone in their fielding positions, with total attention to getting the balls that are hit as if they were in a game situation. Kids love to kibbitz, but in learning situations such as these, it is up to the coach to see that everyone is working and paying attention.

I hear many young players complain about being tired, and I wonder how this can be. The only time I ever felt tired was sitting on the bench and not playing. Whenever we had an off day, I would come to the park and take some hitting because during the season I was unhappy not playing. My rookie year with the Twins in 1961 didn't leave me any time for that. I played a seventy-game season in Puerto Rico, a month in the Dominican Republic, and then a week later I was in Orlando for spring training and playing a full season with the Twins.

I won't say that a person can't get tired but often fatigue is mental, and the mind can play crazy tricks on the body and convince it of something that may not be true. It is the same when guys get in a slump for a couple of days. Right away, they say they are tired and need a couple of days off. Probably what they need are a couple of good hitting sessions to get their timing back. It's amazing what happens to a tired body once the ball begins to fly off the bat!

However, players must also conserve their energies for the game. Running two or three miles on the day of a game isn't really smart because it saps the body of energy needed for the game. We have players in the big leagues who do that nearly every day, and then when July and August come around, they complain about being tired. They probably are, but it's not from playing baseball. Every player can get enough pregame exercise with the regimen I outlined earlier in this chapter, and be in good shape to play every game. Save the heavy work for the off-season as part of a plan to stay in shape when there are no games to be played.

The one area where fatigue can play a negative role is when a player overdoes his hitting; that may sound like a contradiction since I have been advocating getting as much as possible, but do it over a reasonable period of time and allow your muscles to rejuvenate. A fifteen- or twenty-minute minimum period is fine, and then your body will tell you when to stop. My hands and my shoulders used to tell me and I'd stop. Don't be macho and try to fight through something like this because fatigue breeds bad habits—slow hands or a lazy swing, and pretty soon all the work to perk up that timing is lost and the bad habits reappear. Once you hit a series of pitches—five or six, perhaps—right on the nose, then you know you have a good groove. That's a good time to stop, particularly if you have been working for a while to get that good groove.

Selecting a Bat

When you select a bat, let your hands be the judge, and by all means, don't pay attention to the name on the barrel. What is good for a major league player may be all wrong for a youngster.

When I played for the Twins, I used two bats. Against left-handed pitchers I used a K55 because it had a bigger head and knob and gave me enough wood to feel confident that if I got jammed I could still hit the pitch. It was 35 inches long and weighed 34 ounces. Against right-handed pitchers I used a D2, which was 35 inches long and weighed 33 ounces. I could see the ball better against righties so I felt more comfortable and confident usuing a skinnier, lighter bat, and I got more home run power from it.

As a point of information—and maybe to contradict some old theories—many home run hitters use light bats, not big war clubs. Harmon Killebrew, one of the greatest home run hitters in baseball history who was a teammate of mine with the Twins, used a bat that was 35 inches long but ony 31 or 32 ounces, and it looked like a yardstick as he held it in his massive hands. It had a skinny handle that he could whip around with ease and a big head that would just explode the ball into the far reaches of any ballpark in the American League.

One year, I went to a 37-ounce bat because I thought I could get more wood on every pitch, but that was stupid and I wound up not getting much wood on anything. Not only that, but I hurt my shoulder and arms trying to swing that tree, so by mid-season I was back to my regular models. If there is any such thing as a rule, I recommend a 33- to 35-ounce bat for big guys who can hammer the ball. Kirby Puckett, for example uses those sizes and the balls really jump off his bat. I'm amazed sometimes when I see 230-pound guys using a 31-or 32-ounce bat because they say it gives them greater speed. How can guys that big not produce enough speed with a heavier bat?

As I noted, the final selection is up to your hands—how they feel when the bat nestles atop the fingers. Kent Hrbek uses a 31- or 32-ounce bat, and he also hits a lot of balls out of sight. If you use a bat weighing 35 ounces, generally there will not be as much wood in the head because the handle is thicker as opposed to a 33- or 34-ounce model which will have more wood at the top.If you are a home-run hitter, use a bat with a skinny handle, because it will be quicker going around and quicker in your hands. Smaller guys who are control hitters and who depend on banging the ball to opposite fields should use a bat with a bigger handle and bigger head for easier control, since the hitter is not going to be whipping it around for power.

Don't get too caught up in this matter of bat speed. For one thing, bat speed doesn't come from a bat; it comes from the player, so it really doesn't matter whether the bat is 31 or 33 or 34 ounces as long as you can get it around and be quick.

However, if there is indecision, then go with a lighter bat, because it will not hamper your swing as much as the heavier models. Young players can use bats up to 33 inches in length; they will usually weigh less than 30 ounces. But once they begin to move into semi-pro or pro levels, then they sould add a couple of inches to get full plate coverage. In both cases, that piece of wood should feel confortable.

One of the biggest changes is the prolific use of aluminum bats at all but the minor and major league levels. Players coming from high school and college into professional baseball often have more problems adjusting to wooden bats than adjusting to pitchers because they may go from a bat weighing about 30 ounces to a wooden model that weighs up to 35 ounces. Five ounces may not sound like much until you start trying to get it around on a pitch coming ninety miles per hour. I once tried to hit with an aluminum bat, and I couldn't hit very well because I didn't have a good feel for the stick. I can understand the problems of players going from aluminum to wood.

But aluminum bats are here to stay because of the economics involved. They don't break, so it saves money for programs that don't have a lot of money. Therefore, the players must learn to adapt. I suggest to high school kids that they use a 31-ounce, 31- to 33-inch-long aluminum model, but if they are fortunate enough to be in a program that utilizes wooden bats, then they should go up a couple of ounces. One of the problems of switching to wooden bats is that your hands bear more punishment when the ball is struck, and they become sore after a while.

III. Gripping And Choking The Bat

A hitter's bat is his best friend... and then comes his hitting coach. After that, everyone else can stand in line.

I'm certain you have heard stories of batters on hot streaks who took their bats home and slept with them so they wouldn't cool off or of hitters who borrowed bats from teammates, caught a hot hitting streak, and then wouldn't give the bats back.

That is why a bat becomes a prized possession for every hitter, but you must remember one thing: A bat is only a piece of wood. What you do with it, and how you do it, makes it special.

The Grip

We've already talked about how to select a bat, but once you have it, then what? The first thing is to learn how to hold it properly, in other words, how to grip it. There are many who think the best way to grip a bat is to almost strangle it in your hands... to hold it so tightly that the knob almost jumps off from the pressure. Nothing could be worse.

The first step is to hold the bat loosely on the tips of the fingers, away from the palm of the hand. You should make your grip firm as the pitcher delivers the ball, and not while waiting in the batter's box. The only hitter I ever knew who held the bat in the palms of his hands was Harmon Killebrew, my teammate on the Twins who now is in the Hall of Fame after hitting more than 500 lifetime home runs.

Oops, you might say. Doesn't that mean something?

Not really, because Harmon was an unusual hitter who had thick hands and not especially graceful fingers. It was uncomfortable for him to lay a bat on his fingertips and attempt to grip it. Thus, he slid it down into his palms where he had firm control and could expend so much power.

I'd say about 95 percent of all major league hitters hold their bats on theirfingertips, not only for control but also to provide a cushion against bone bruises on hands that can occur when they are jammed by tight pitches. When the ball strikes the lower part of the handle, it forces the bat back into the hands, and unless there is a space for it to recoil, it lands against the bone area between the thumb and

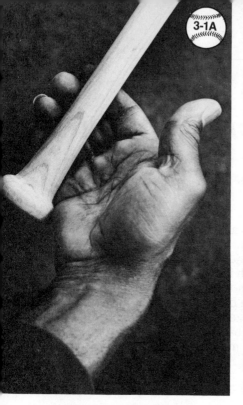

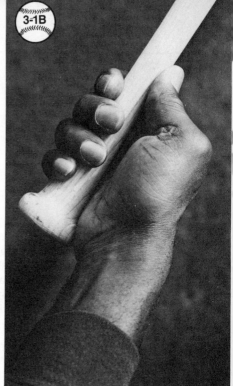

USING THE FINGER TIPS:
Gripping the bat begins by holding the bat on the finger tips on the bottom hand, photo 3-1A, before closing the hand firmly, as shown in photo 3-1B. Repeat the process for the top hand, in photos 3-1C and 3-1D, and then grasp the bat firmly in both hands, photo 3-1E. Allow your fingers to wrap naturally around the handle.

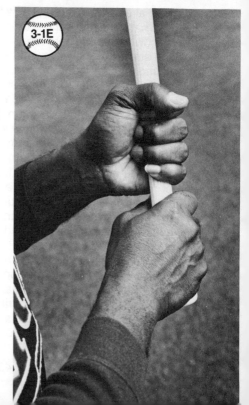

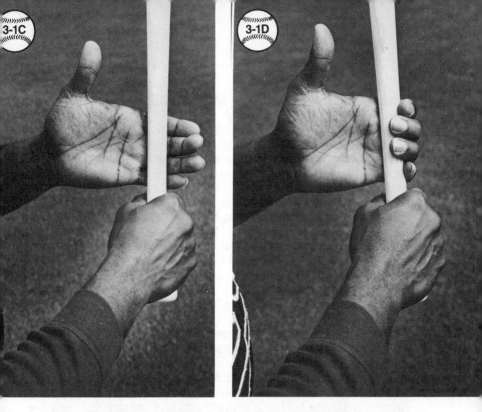

forefinger. This happens to many young players who think they must grip the bat deeply in their hands, and the results are sore hands that may keep them from swinging their bats for a few games.

If you hold the bat on the fingertips you'll get a better, more comfortable grip that will provide more power and also allow for greater hand quickness when you swing. The top hand, which controls the swing, must be able to accurately direct the bat, and this cannot be done efficiently if the bat is deep in the palm. Fingertip control will give you added precision. I also found that holding the bat on my fingertips gave me a strong grip—certainly at least as strong as those who grabbed the bat deeper in their hands and lost the other benefits from greater hand control.

I always get some negative reaction when I lay a bat on the fingertips of a young hitter and tell him to grasp the bat.

"I won't be able to control it," is the biggest early complaint.

"Sure you will," I always assure them. "Just be certain that your fingers can go around the bat."

"But I use a big bat," one player might complain.

"No problem," I would say. "You can still hold it with both hands and not lose anything."

"But I use a skinny handled bat," another player might say.

"Don't you worry, either," I would reply. "If you use a skinny handle, hold the bat in your fingertips. When you close your hand, it will not move toward the back of your hands and you'll have perfect bat control."

The big thing, I tell both groups, is that when they hit the ball, the bat will not be driven backward but will go forward in a steady motion. It is only when the bat lies deeper in your hands that it can be driven backward into the soft fleshy parts near the thumb and forefinger, with, as I noted, a good case of sore hands. You may want to check your grip by aligning the second knuckles of your top hand either between the knuckles closest to the hand and second knuckle or closer to the second knuckles. However, never lineup the second knuckles of the top hand with the knuckles closest to the hand; this puts the bat in the palms of both hands and restricts the wrist and arm action in the swing.

Of course, I also am asked so often why bats go flying out of the hands of hitters after they swing the bat. It happened to me many times during my major league career, particularly on the first or second swings because I was looser and more relaxed. When I faced a two-strike count, I concentrated more on hitting the ball hard, adjusted my stance in the batter's box, and probably unconsciously held the bat a bit tighter so I would make good contact.

I'm not bothered by hitters losing control of their bats and seeing them fly onto the field or backward into foul territory. Probably the only people who really mind are the fielders or the pitcher who suddenly find a bat bearing down on them, or guys in the dugout who aren't paying attention to the game and suddenly get a rude awakening as a bat comes flying into their lives.

Often, bats fly because hitters get badly fooled by a pitcher and are totally out of control as they swing; most flying bats come on good breaking pitches. I'll give that to the pitcher, but that is where it ends. If you have two strikes, be certain to hold the bat tighter if for no other reason than to keep control and not strike out. Do that, and the ball, not the bat, will go flying.

In gripping the bat, the key is to be consistent. Don't change grips because the other team changes pitchers. Use one grip for every pitcher, right-handed or left-handed. And don't experiment with different grips. Find one that is comfortable and stay with it. When you get into a slump, the grip is rarely to blame. Remember, you can only do so much with your hands.

Here are some tips on how to get the perfect grip:

1. Be certain that after you have the bat lying in your fingertips, your knuckles are lined up when you close your hands around it. The second knuckles of the top hand are either in alignment with the second knuckles of the bottom hand, or are somewhere between the

3-2

ALIGNMENT OF THE KNUCKLES
The second knuckles on the fingers of the hand should align somewhere between the second knuckles and the back knuckles of the bottom hand, as in photo 3-2; avoid aligning the back knuckles of the hands, as this restricts the hand and wrist action.

second knuckles and knuckles closest to the hand of the bottom hand.

2. Don't roll either hand over so far that the back knuckles of both hands are aligned.

3. Be certain your hands are four to five inches in front of you and in alignment with your rear foot and knee—about three to four inches to the rear of your back knee.

4. Hold the bat firmly, but do not squeeze the bat too tightly. This creates excessive contraction of the muscles and tension. You should be alert but relaxed when you start the swing. You have plenty of time to tighten your grip as the pitcher delivers the ball.

I am asked frequently about hitters who use interlocking grips, where the fingers on the top hand become entwined with the top digits of the bottom hand. Some use this comfortably and if that is the case, and they are successful, then that is good for them. We had a hitter on the Twins who held the knob of the bat with the thumb and forefinger, and the rest of the bottom hand hung free below the knob.

One day I said to him, "Why don't you use your entire hand?"

"It feels more comfortable this way," he replied.

I just shook my head and walked away because the player was a producer, so why should he change?

Choking Up

I choked up on my bat all the time, but particularly after the pitcher had two strikes in the count. And just to make certain that I did it on the right place on my bat, I placed a little piece of tape about a half inch up the handle. That was my reference point. And you know, Kirby Puckett on our club now does the same thing, only his tape is almost an inch up the bat.

I say that about Puckett because there are many with the mistaken notion that choking up on the bat robs a hitter of power or is a mark of weakness when facing a good pitcher. Both are nonsense, and I'll tell you why choking up is not all that bad.

1. Holding the bat a half inch or even an inch up the handle gives the hitter a better chance to hit the ball on the best part of the bat, getting all of the good wood on his pitch.

2. It also provides more confidence to the hitter because he knows he will have better control of the bat.

In that regard, it amazes me when big league hitters suddenly become more productive once they begin to choke up. It happens on

MARK THE CHOKE-UP SPOT:
Find a spot on the bat that is comfortable when you choke up and as in photo 3-3, mark it with a strip if tape that will indicate where you will place your bottom hand.

our own club, and I'll say to them, "Why didn't you do that at the beginning? You're still hitting line drives and getting your home runs."

So, don't wait for a slump or a problem. Choke up a bit from the time you begin to hit and enjoy all of the advantages. And don't be misled by what some big league players do. I can't understand guys with four or five years of major league experience who still wait until they get two strikes and then get their hits. Maybe they are just stubborn—or dumb—and simply refuse to realize they never need get themselves in a hole.

Who Should Choke Up?

Nearly every hitter should come up on the bat a bit, but hitters without much power, who must rely on bat control and the ability to guide the ball to different fields, should choke up, and so should line drive hitters and home run hitters. The idea of batting is to get a hit, and the more you do it, the more you play. Players who don't produce and who insist on holding the bat at the very end are being foolish and deserve to lose their starting roles.

A good example of a power hitter who is not afraid to choke up is Jose Canseco of the Oakland A's, who led the major leagues in home runs in 1988. Another, as I noted, is Kirby Puckett, who has accumulated more than 1,000 hits, including 273 extra base hits, in just five major league seasons.

Power hitters can do it. They are strong enough to get the ball out, and with better bat control from choking up a bit, they will do it more consistently. And they will do it without having to use oversize bats. Greg Gagne on the Twins uses a small bat, and he hit fourteen home runs in 1988. I played with a big, strong player named Ted Uhlander, who did not have a great deal of power despite his size. Using a big bat and choking up, he became a very good line drive hitter who was nearly always around the .300 mark. Another good example is Felix Milan, who made a long career for himself in the big leagues because he learned to choke up on the bat and get his hits consistently.

Choking up does not indicate a weakness to the pitcher. I never cared what the pitchers thought about me when I came up a half inch on the bat, and I got my hits. Then I knew what they were thinking about me. A lot of young players think they can stay down on the handle and bulldoze a pitcher, or frighten him. Nonsense. That is nothing but false pride, and a batter's foolish, false pride can be a pitcher's best friend.

Forget about pride. Worry more about getting a good swing and hitting the ball than how you will look if you swing and miss with the bat gripped next to the knob. Sometimes you have to concede something to a great pitcher by coming up on the bat, but so what? If you get a hit against him, then you have won the battle.

What does choking up on the bat do for the swing? If a hitter chokes up from the time he begins playing baseball, he will improve his hitting much more quickly. Consider the following:

1. It gives you more concentration, even if you are a big, strong hitter.

2. If you're small, you're not going to hit a lot of home runs anyhow, but choking up will give you better balance and an ability to hit the ball on the best part of the bat.

3. You'll get more line drive hits and hit the ball hard to all parts of the field. The result can easily be a good number of extra base hits during the season.

4. You won't get jammed as much, and instead of foul balls or dribblers coming from those inside pitches, balls can be zinging to the outfield as base hits. More base hits—and fewer dribblers—mean more playing time. On the major league level, guys who can produce a lot of hits—and not necessarily a lot of home runs— can also produce some good salary figures.

5. It lessens the amount of distance the bat must travel, giving a hitter a shorter, more compact swing. The result is more concentration, particularly at two strikes, on hitting the ball.

All of this brings me to what young players should be doing—at all the lower levels of competition they should be swinging the bat. Little and junior league coaches only inhibit the growth of young players by sending them to the plate and telling them to get a walk. Tell them to get a hit instead, and give them the confidence that you believe they can do it.

Still, young hitters often are intimidated by strong pitchers who they believe throw fast enough to overpower them. That will never change, regardless of the level of competition, because good fastball pitchers are always going to come with that pitch in key situations. If a hitter gets ahead 2-0 in the count, he can always expect to see a fastball from a good, smart fastball pitcher. So if it means coming up on the bat to handle a pitch he knows is coming, then by all means he should do it.

Even in the big leagues I am astounded when hitters come back to the dugout and moan about "not expecting a fastball" at critical counts when they are facing a fastball pitcher. Why in the world would they be looking for a breaking pitch when they had the pitcher in a hole?

Now, I am not saying that if you are an extraordinary hitter and truly believe that a fastball pitcher is coming with his best heat, you can't go down to the end of the bat and get as much power behind your swing as possible. If you do, be sure to concentrate and go for that pitch.

But for most other hitters, don't be afraid to choke up—on the bat, not in the game.

IV. The Stance

So often a hitter's trademark is his stance at the plate.

Certainly, major league hitters are so visible that young players are totally familiar with players like Wade Boggs, who seem to drape themselves over the plate, or others like Mark McGwire of the Oakland A's, who seem to stand erect with a classic pose that is so natural for big, power hitters, or still others like George Brett of the Kansas City Royals, who stand well back in the batter's box.

It is not unusual for young hitters to try to copy their favorite players in every detail, including their stance, without realizing that it may not be helpful to their own hitting ability. That is why a young player must develop his own trademarks, including his own stance. It is so important to be yourself at the plate and to go after the ball in a way that is most natural to your talent and your physical makeup. In other words, don't form bad habits based on what someone else does successfully.

For example, Brett is certainly one of baseball's premier hitters. Standing back in the box, he can hit the ball to left field any time he wants, even though he is a left-handed batter, and he can smoke it to right field. You may see him release his top hand when he hits the ball, and while that may be fine for him, if you try it, you won't be able to hit as well. The key, then, is to do what you do best and what is comfortable for you.

Now, having said that, let's look at five good rules to develop the proper foot position in the batter's box, the basis for developing a good batting stance:

1. Take your time getting into the box. Don't be hurried. I always took my time, and I'm sure it made some pitchers mad, but so what? I was the batter and I had to be comfortable, otherwise I would have given that pitcher an edge.

2. Be certain that your spikes are clean and that they will help you get a secure and firm position with your feet.

3. Be sure that any uneven gravel or dirt is smoothed out and that you will have a level or comfortable platform under your feet. Even in the major leagues, I see hitters who are careless about what may seem to be a minor thing but nonetheless big enough to disrupt their balance and cause them to foul off pitches or prevent them from getting a good swing.

PLATE COVERAGE: *After getting comfortable in a closed, open or square stance, make sure you can cover the entire plate by first extending the bat with your lower hand so that it touches the outside of the plate as in photos 4-4A, 4-5A, 4-6A. From any of those stances, take a practice swing, photos 4-4B, 4-5B, 4-6B, to assure yourself that you have full plate coverage.*

4. Plant your back foot properly, because the power in your stride will begin from that foot. You may want to dig a small "toe hole."

5. Don't stand either too close or too far from the plate, but above all be certain that your bat will cover the entire plate area. Extend the bat with your bottom hand and touch the outside of the plate; this will let you know that you can reach all strikes. You will know that anything over any part of the plate can be hit, and thus, you will have more confidence.

Width of the Stance

Everyone is different, which is one reason why I said at the outset not to mimic any particular big league player. When I started playing baseball, I had a very wide open stance and I took a short stride. Later in the big leagues after I saw how the pitchers were working on me, I shortened my stance, particularly when I got well ahead in the count, but if I got behind by two strikes, I widened out even more and concentrated on hitting down on the ball. By widening out, I was not as much of a standup target, hence my strike zone shrank somewhat. I also had to forget about hitting the long ball and concentrate more on hitting the ball hard someplace else on the field.

Thus, I knew I was in better control of my bat and that I could probably hit anything the pitcher threw to me. My concentration was better, and I forced the pitcher to work harder because I lowered the strike zone. My balance also was better because I was lower, the strike zone was easier to cover, and I had better bat control because I didn't have to stride as far with my front foot.

For young players, the width of their stance should be such that they can comfortably swing without striding too far with the front foot and without finding they are so spread out that when they do stride, nothing much happens. One of the best ways, of course, is to take a bat, and stand in front of a mirror and look at your stance. At the same time, decide for yourself whether it feels natural and comfortable. Then take a few swings to see how it looks. By seeing and feeling, you can adjust what you are doing and make a visual comparison between the old and the new. Thus, if you ever get into a slump, you can stand in front of that mirror again and recall what the comfortable stance looked like versus what the current stance may be like.

I offer this as a good remedy for problems in any part of the batting routine—hands, arms, legs, whatever—because you get a full-faced view of yourself as you should be. Swing the bat, watch the hands, the feet, and the hips, and then see where you may have gone astray.

The more you do that when you are, the better frames of reference you will have when there are problems.

Also, don't be misled by advice that your feet should be spread no wider than your shoulders. Instead, you should stand at the plate in a way that makes you most comfortable and makes you a productive hitter. If you don't have a good, comfortable stance, then you won't be able to produce. Soon, you'll find you may take too long a stride, thus moving your entire body and causing your eyes to move off the path of the ball.

Start with the weight on the back foot, and on the ball of that foot, not on the heel. That will give you better balance and allow you to wait longer for breaking pitches. Remember, not every pitch you see is going to be a fastball, and you can always stride into that pitch, but if you get a curve, the weight on your back foot allows you time to switch the weight from the back to the front and snap the bat with some power. If your weight is resting on your front foot, it is difficult to stride into the pitch, and all you really can do is hit the ball with your hands.

I've watched plenty of films of great hitters, and almost without exception their weight is on the back foot at the start of the swing. You can see them waiting on the pitch and then moving that weight from the back to the front foot as they begin to stride. Remember, you don't want to get fooled too often with different kinds of breaking pitches—there is more than one kind of curveball, you know—so with the weight back, you'll have a better chance to succeed.

The power you produce will come from the back foot and go directly to the front foot. To do this, be sure your rear foot is firmly planted, even if you have to dig a small hole, so that you will have something from which to push forward. Then, when the time comes, there is a conscious move from the back foot to the front, yet that back foot still is in place when you finish your swing, giving you good balance for your follow-through.

Take only an 8-inch or less stride. If you have a short stride, you will have better balance and as I noted before, your head and your eyes will not move that much. That keeps your concentration on the ball after it leaves the pitcher's hand, and you will have it always in sight as you swing the bat. If you take a big stride with the front foot, your head will also move a greater distance, and by the time you steady your head again, the pitch will be on top of you.

How should you adjust your feet, once you've found a comfortable stance? Don't try to stride in different directions to hit various kinds of pitches or to place the ball in specific areas of the outfield. If you want to adjust to pitches or to pitchers, then you move *both* feet to a different position prior to the delivery of the pitch. I know some kids often are told to point a foot or draw it back in a special position to hit to the opposite field, but all that does is throw off your stride. For example, if you alter just your rear foot—such as by moving it closer to the plate—and not the front one, then you may not be able to handle an inside pitch against a hard-throwing pitcher because he will be able to jam you with inside fastballs. But if you adjust both feet, such as by moving back in the box a bit against the same hard-throwing pitcher—which puts you a little further away from where you must meet the ball and thus allows for an easier full extension of your arms—you will have more time and be able to hit that inside pitch.

Let me repeat the point about not mimicking famous hitters. Wade Boggs of the Red Sox has a beautiful stance for his particular style of hitting. When you watch him work before the game, you know that ninety percent of the time he wants to hit the ball to the opposite field. Pitchers will work him inside to try to get him to pull the ball, so he adjusts his stance to take those pitches the other way. He leans out over the plate, unlike some power hitters who stand more erect. This works for him, but only because he knows he wants to hit to the opposite field. I believe Wade is a good enough hitter that he can hit 20 home runs a year and still bat .350 if he wants—he proved that in 1987 when he hit 24 and also won the American League batting title with a .363 mark—but at this point, he seems more content to concentrate on hitting the ball to the opposite field.

Can any young hitter do this? Not really, because they simply may not be comfortable at the plate making all the necessary foot adjustments to take those balls all over the park. Wade Boggs certainly would not be comfortable standing more erect at the plate and trying to pull the ball to right field most of the time.

Type of Stance

Now that you've decided where your feet should be, you have to decide whether you want an open, closed, or square stance. In the open stance the front foot is pointed away from the center of the field at an approximate forty-five degree angle to an imaginary line drawn from the toes of your back foot to the pitcher. In the closed stance your front foot points toward the opposite field and is somewhat forward of a line drawn from the toes of your back foot to the pitcher. A closed stance always has your front foot closer to the plate. In the square stance your feet are parallel to the inside line of the batter's box, or to an imaginary line from the back point of home plate to the pitcher. A parallel stance always has your feet equidistant from the plate. I don't advocate one over the other as a particular rule of thumb, but I do believe young hitters should open their stance to the

OPEN STANCE: The front foot is pointed away from the center of the field at a slight angle, as in photo 4-1.

THE CLOSED STANCE: The front foot is always closer to the plate, photo 4-2, and points to the opposite field.

THE SQUARE STANCE: Photo 4-3 shows both feet parallel to the inside line of the batter's box.

point where they are comfortable and can get maximum production from their hitting.

Practice using different stances. I had two or three myself, one for the times I faced a left-handed pitcher, one against a right-hander, and one when I wished to pull the ball. Against a lefty, I liked to be close to the plate with my back foot almost behind it. I was open, and that way I could see the pitcher's hands a lot more clearly and pick up the pitch as soon as he released it. If a lefty tries to throw a fastball inside, or a slider in the middle of the plate or even away, and you are close to the plate and open a little bit, then you'll be able to handle it. And don't be afraid of getting jammed. You can't be a good hitter and fear the inside pitch. It is better to be jammed than to strike out. Learn to handle the inside pitch by developing quick hands, so the pitcher will never get an edge on you. And don't take those kinds of pitches too personally or get mad. That is part of the pitcher's game, and he is entitled to come inside on you. You must learn how to handle it. Hall of Famer Ted Williams, one of the greatest left-handed hitters in baseball history, recognized how important it is for a hitter to be quick as possible on inside pitches this is why he stressed being quick with the hips, because once the hips are cleared, the arm and hands and bat can accelerate through the hitting area.

When I faced a right-handed pitcher who also threw hard, I'd give him all of home plate. Then I could hit him up the middle or to the opposite field and not have to pull everything. Remember, I was a left-handed batter so I was getting many pitches inside. If I saw a righty who did not throw too hard, I got closer to the plate and then I'd try to pull the ball if I got that kind of good pitch.

The only time I altered my stance was when I was in a slump, and then I did it so that I could hit the ball to the opposite field by moving back from the plate a little bit. That's about all I did. Once I got a couple of hits, I had my confidence back and I was ready to adjust myself to the various pitchers and go back to using my regular stances.

Remember, in moving back from the plate, move both feet but particularly the back foot. If the front foot is too close, move that also. When you are back, you will be able to take any pitch to the opposite field without thinking about it.

And the less you have to think about when you are hitting, the more hits you are apt to get.

V. Striding Your Way To A Better Average

I'll bet that people watching a hitter always focus on the action of the bat and the swing and rarely watch the upper part of the hitter's body. That's too bad because what happens from the hips to the ground makes all the difference in the world to what happens with the bat and the swing.

That's why I always tell hitters that they can stride their way to a higher batting average—and note that I said *stride,* not swing. I certainly don't want to down play the importance of a good swing— we will devote an entire chapter later in this book to that one subject—but good hitting begins with the lower part of the body, and hitters who do not work hard to achieve sound, fundamental action down there will not do much with their bat.

Let me try to prove my point before I go into further details. Grab a bat, or a stick of some kind, and take your hitting stance. Now, swing as if you are about to hit a pitch.

What happened? Did you swing without moving your front foot? Do you even remember moving your front foot? You did, you know, because that's the only way to begin the power surge that enables you to swing the bat and hit the ball.

Let's do that again, only this time, when you swing, make a conscious effort not to move your front foot.

What happened? You got a sort of herky-jerky, off-balance motion with your upper body that would have produced little or no power and a pretty sad-looking bat swing. Even if you actually hit a ball swinging this way, it wouldn't go very far.

All of this is to show you why I spend so much time talking about the stride and why it is so important. For one thing, if you stride properly, you will be less likely to get fooled on a pitch. That should be reason enough to master this phase of hitting because the less you get fooled, the more hits you get and the higher your average will soar.

Okay, all hitters want big averages but let's get to a more serious reason. When you stride properly, you move your entire body in a perfectly balanced way that all good hitters strive to achieve. You step toward the pitcher, keeping the toes of the front foot as close as possible to perpendicular to the imaginary line from the plate to the pitcher. Do not turn the toes toward the pitcher, as this will open the hips too soon.

Keep in mind that *only* the front foot should move. Plant that rear foot and keep it planted because when moving or striding with the front foot, that firmly planted back foot will supply the power for your move. Push against the ground with the ball of your rear foot. This will keep it planted and help accelerate the opening of your hips as you swing.

How Long Should You Stride?

Young players, particularly, are always trying to be comfortable in the batter's box and look for the perfect motion with their body and bat. Thus, the right kind of stride is one that is short, perhaps no more than eight inches. Young players are often surprised when I tell them this. They believe that to become big power hitters they must take a big step into the pitch and bash the ball out of sight. What will most likely happen if they do that is a pop up or a flying bat because their entire body will be out of rhythm.

Think back to the times you have seen little guys jerk a ball out of the park. You'll never see them take a big stride. They can't, but they certainly take one that is long enough to supply the power to hit a home run.

Okay, we know that if you stride no more than eight inches, you'll be doing okay. But when you do, be certain that your front foot always moves in a direct line toward the pitcher, always keeping your body in balance and your hips closed until you commit to swinging. If your front foot moves too far toward the plate when you stride, your hips will close further, your shoulder and elbows will drop, and you will have great difficulty getting your hands and bat to the hitting area. If that front foot moves too far away from the plate, you'll find your body rising up and your hips opening too soon, often locking your arms too close to your body and producing a very weak swing.

Striding properly is not easy. It takes a great deal of practice, in and out of the batter's box, to find a move that is comfortable and allows you to keep a good hitting style. One easy way to develop the right stride is to place a bat or a stick at a distance that feels comfortable and then practice stepping just that far. If you do this drill consistently, your body will become tuned to the proper distance. After a while, it will become such a natural move that you'll hardly even give it a thought. If you overstride, it is more difficult to keep your hands back, ready to launch the bat, as the hands tend to come forward in a long stride. This produces a slow, weak swing.

SETTING YOUR STRIDE: *Get comfortable in the batter's box and mark a spot by your front foot, photo 5-1A. Then move as if to hit the ball, and mark a spot, by drawing a line in the dirt, or placing a stick, at the furthest point of your stride, photo 5-1B. For the player of average height, the distance should never be more than 12 inches. Here, Tony Oliva found his stride to be 8 inches.*

I also recommend that you get someone to determine just how you are striding. Have him check the distance and how it affects your body. He will see whether you are out of balance, and the two of you can work to get just the proper distance.

Keep That Front Foot "Quiet"

A proper striding technique with the front foot means that it will move quietly just above the ground in the batter's box. We say "quietly" because it should be barely noticeable, almost a sliding motion rather than a raised step movement. Kirby Puckett often raises his front foot quite a bit when he strides but that is only good for him because he is comfortable with it. I always want hitters doing first what they find comfortable and second what will help them be

QUIET STRIDE: The front foot should move barely above the ground, photo 5-2, almost a sliding motion.

THE PUCKETT STRIDE: Batters who raise their front foot when they stride, as in photo 5-3, can also be successful. Some hitters find that this unorthodox style works very well in keeping their weight back before committing to step and swing.

good hitters. So don't think you can copy Kirby Puckett's style and be successful. He does other things when he swings to compensate for that foot movement, and many hitters are simply unable to copy them.

The Hips Will Follow

Much has been said and written about the proper hip action in hitting a baseball. Ted Williams is always preaching about the importance of proper hip movement, and he based much of his hitting theory on this action. I completely agree with him, and in fact, I often went to him when I was in a slump and had him straighten out what I knew were faulty hip motions in my own batting technique.

I mention the hip action because the stride of the front foot toward the pitcher initiates the sequence of body actions that eventually opens up the hips. But I don't want young hitters worrying so much about what will happen with the hip motion that they forget everything else. If you stride properly, you will open your hips sufficiently to hit the ball. That's not to say that changes in hip motion aren't necessary sometimes. For instance, if a pull hitter has had trouble making contact, I would have him open his stance a bit, get closer to the plate, and be very quick with the bat.

But all of this will come with experience, and young hitters should not become so wrapped up in what is happening to their hips that they lose track of how they are striding. Work on the stride, concentrate on it, keeping it consistent and as short as is comfortable to you. Once you learn to do that, you can graduate to the "hip level" where you can work on some of the "tricks of the hitting trade" that will enable you to do more with your bat.

Staying Down and Transferring the Weight

The striding motion is important, and I want young hitters to flex their front knee and to stay down as they move and plant that front foot. The front leg will naturally straighten momentarily during the swing when the weight is fully transferred and the ball is struck. This slight downward motion in the stride will keep the hips from opening too soon. It will also keep the front shoulder from opening too soon, the hands back, and the head and eyes directed into the eventual hitting zone. Once the front foot is planted and the batter commits to swing, the hip action will naturally pull the front shoulder up and out as it exchanges position with the rear shoulder. If a hitter does not start with this slight downward motion, the body will tend to fly

STRIDE RIGHT: *The front foot must stride in a straight line toward the pitcher with the toe as closed as possible, photo 5-4A, and 5-4B. Do not open the toe until your weight transfers or you will lose balance, photo 5-5A. A faulty stride will open up the hips too soon and you'll have problems making contact with the ball, 5-5B.*

upward and out of the hitting zone, and the eyes will simply lose sight of the ball. If a player can't follow the ball, he certainly won't be able to hit it, and as I noted earlier, it is very difficult to find the ball again in a split second.

Earlier in this chapter I said that you should keep the rear foot firmly planted in the batter's box. That's where your weight will be before you begin your stride and swing. The key rule to remember when transferring the weight from your back foot to your front foot is that the bat should meet the ball when the weight is transferred to the front foot. When perfectly timed, you will hit the ball with authority and power.

Young hitters often get caught up on weight transfer just as they do on hips, so I am not going to give an inch-by-inch description of exactly what happens. I will tell you that if you do not transfer your weight properly, your bat may be well out in front of the pitch, and your timing will be off. Thus you will:

1. not hit the ball solidly;
2. find your bat flying out of your hands when you miss a breaking ball; and
3. get too far in front of the pitch.

The proper technique, then, is to keep that weight back on the rear foot until you decide to swing at the ball. If it is a fastball, move quicker. If it is a breaking pitch, hesitate slightly before transferring your weight, but in both instances, once committed, move your weight from the rear to the front hip as you swing as quickly as possible. Again, if you make the swing at the right time, you'll never have to worry about your hips because the power switch will happen as you move.

Let me say something to young hitters who always worry about hitting breaking pitches. (If you can't hit a fastball, then you won't have much of a baseball career.) Take as much batting practice as possible against breaking pitches and work on your timing so that you'll be able to make that power switch in one smooth motion. The more breaking balls you see, the more you will learn about keeping your weight back and then getting the power going at just the right time from back to front. The end result will be a consistent swing.

Play a lot of pepper, a game in which you have to be quick with the bat. Put yourself into a game situation when doing this and you will develop the quickness of moving your weight from back to front and accelerating the bat with a flick of the wrists. Above all, don't play pepper with just the arms doing the work because you aren't improving yourself at all.

There's one other thing. When you have your weight on your rear foot, bend your knees slightly. This will help generate the power that will enable you to shift your weight to the front. It will also be easier if you have to get out of the way of a pitch or adjust on a breaking ball or try to pull a ball. If your knees are stiff, you will lose that flexibility to adjust to the pitches.

One More Time

So what have we done? We have put you in the batter's box, in a comfortable stance, and have told you to take a step, no longer than eight inches, in a straight line toward the pitcher as you swing at the ball. Your bat should meet the ball immediately after you make this step, ideally as your weight transfers from the rear foot to the front foot.

Long hours of practice are so necessary to perfect this move and will keep that stride in perfect balance. Your eyes, shoulders, hips, and hands will all work together in making those base hits come true.

VI. It's All In The Hands

I cannot emphasize too strongly the importance of the hands in hitting a baseball. Not only are the hands used to grip and choke up on the bat as we discussed in Chapter III, but they help to swing it. How the batter uses his hands in the swing will determine much of how successful he will be in getting base hits or consistently driving the ball beyond the infield. However, many hitters, particularly young hitters, take their hands for granted. They give little thought to exactly what they must do and less still to how improper use of the hands can badly affect their ability to hit.

We have heard in recent years some hitting theories that say the top hand should leave the bat before the follow-through is completed. Before we begin our discussion on the proper use of the hands, let me say right out that I disagree. A batter's hands should never leave the bat until the entire follow-through process has been completed. Occasionally, it will happen, but this should only be accidental and only after leaving the impact area of the swing. Players who exaggerate the hand-release technique can easily fall into sloppy habits and lose that sensitive bat control that is so vital to getting base hits. The release of the top hand is a misconception of the late Charley Lau's teaching. Lau often had players practice releasing the top hand to emphasize full extension, which produces the hardest hit balls. I advocate full extension too but try to get the players to achieve it with both hands on the bat.

Each hand has a specific function in hitting. The bottom hand pulls the bat through the swing, and the top hand provides bat speed and keeps the bat in control and balance. They must also work as a team, and if they don't, a hitter will soon know he has some problems.

The biggest problem is called a "slow bat," and this is caused by a "slow hand." It simply means that the top hand is not moving fast enough to drive the bat, and a hitter starts missing pitches that he would normally handle easily. Those problems are easy for you to recognize: a mediocre pitch on the corner of the plate gets you out or an inside pitch causes you to get jammed. Pretty soon, the only pitch you can hit is a slow breaking pitch or a so-so fastball, and you become a juicy target for good fastball pitchers who aren't going to fool around. They'll come at you with their best heat...boom! boom! boom!...and you're gone.

I always classify a slow or lazy hand with a lazy body—and often a lazy hip—and believe me, all of us get both regardless of the level of competition. When I felt lazy in my body during my career, I'd get out to the park early to get the juices flowing and my body responding to new energy. When I got a lazy hand—and it happened maybe three or four times a season—I would do the same thing, this time with extra hitting.

I know it is easier for major league players to cure the problem because we can take all of the extra hitting we wish; we can also study films of ourselves when our hands were moving properly, and we have expert help to get us over the rough spots.

Young players do not have it as easy. Therefore, you have to get out and get someone to work with you for two or three days—and that means making an effort yourself and convincing someone else to work with you. But you must do it to cure the problem, and you do it by getting as many swings as possible and getting back into the good groove.

There are some other ways to cure the problem:

1. Move back from the plate a bit and practice hitting to the opposite field.
2. Get better extension with the bat.
3. Get closer to the plate and make the pitcher come inside to force you to get your hips and hands moving fast.
4. Play pepper where you must be quick with the bat to keep the ball in play.
5. Concentrate on pushing down hard and pivoting the rear foot, and thus accelerating the opening of the hips.
6. And practice mental discipline where you constantly remind yourself, "I must be quick! I must be quick!" Remember, your starting job may depend on just how quickly you cure the problem.

Position of the Hands

Hitters should keep their hands about four to six inches from their body in a comfortable position; when viewed from the side they should appear to be slightly to the rear of the back knee about mid-chest level. I don't like to see hitters with their hands up around their ears or down around their belts, though I do understand that some people are more comfortable in these positions. But remember, if your bat is correctly positioned at the outset, then you will be in a better position to launch the proper swing.

POSITION OF THE HANDS: *The hands serve a specific function in hitting a ball, the bottom hand pulling the bat through the swing, and the top one directing the bat and supplying the power. They must grip the bat firmly, photo 6-1A, and be held about four to six inches from the body so that the rear elbow will be parallel or slightly pointed to the ground, photo 6-1B. The hands also should be in a line just above the outside edge of the rear foot, photo 6-1C, and not held either at shoulder level, or in front of the body.*

If your hands are too close to your body, you will have a tougher time getting good extension with your bat. However, you can move them up or down slightly, if that means being more comfortable.

It is key to have the ability to get the pitch you want. I'm always reminded about the time Kirby Puckett once swung at a pitch from Jack Morris of the Detroit Tigers that was nearly over his head. He moved his hands up there, and he got that ball for a two-run single that helped us win the game. Another time, he reached up and went for a ball that was eye-level and drove it out of the park for a home run.

In each instance, Kirby had his hands in perfect position as the pitcher threw the ball, but because he is exceptionally strong he generated enough speed to go up and get those pitches. Nonetheless, he always starts with his hands in the proper position.

What can happen if your drop your hands too far down? First, you must bring the bat back up and into proper position before you can even swing the bat. The only major league player I can recall doing this successfully was former New York Yankee outfielder Roy White, who played with the Yankees during the sixties and early seventies. Somehow, he was quick enough to get his hands back and locked into position before he swung, and I must admit, I was always amazed at how he could do that and still be a .300 hitter.

Secondly, you will have to move your hands up while you stride, and that can prevent a level swing. If you keep them placed in the middle of your body, there is one less motion you have to worry about. The less extraneous motion you have when you swing, the less room there is for mistakes.

I often have told hitters that baseball is a funny game in that you are trying to hit a little, round white ball that is coming 85 or 90 miles an hour, and you have to do it in what amounts to almost a split second. Therefore, you simply do not have enough time to play around.

Keep Those Hands Quiet

When I was at bat during my major league career, I had a reputation as a player who was a bit fidgety—at least until the pitcher was ready to throw the ball. Then I locked myself into place, my hands were ready—although they were never "dead still"—and I was set to make the one quick move that allowed me to drive the ball.

I point this out because many young players—and some major leaguers, I might add—never stop moving some part of their body, or worse still, their hands and their bat, as the pitcher delivers the ball. If you do that, stop right now. It's okay to have some slight motion before the pitcher delivers the ball. But once the pitcher brings his arm around with the ball, you must be still and ready to launch your swing. Discipline yourself to stay still and ready so you can follow the ball from the instant it leaves the pitcher's hands. Discipline is the key here, and if it takes a constant reminder from your coach to help you achieve it, then have him nip at you on every pitch.

Why am I so insistent on this? If you continue to move your hands when the pitcher is throwing the ball, then you will not have time to get ready to hit it. You must be still and ready so that the only thing you have to do is to stride into the ball. If you are moving, by the time you stop and get locked into position, it may already be too late; at best, you may not get a full swing.

Keep Both Hands on the Bat

I already noted in the beginning of this chapter—and I am going to emphasize it again—that you must keep both hands on the bat when you swing. Otherwise, you will simply lose your bat speed and power.

With a fastball, there is little time for the top hand to release too soon from the bat. Full extension of the arms often comes after you've made contact on a fastball. The slower breaking pitches allow more time for full extension, and sometimes an unintentional top-hand release during follow-through. With a breaking pitch, try to maintain complete control of the bat from start to finish. The hands may stay on the bat all the way through your swing, and you should never consciously try to release that top hand early.

As I also noted, there may be occasions when you're trying to get full extension of the arms—an ideal position for meeting the ball with your bat—and your top hand will fly off. However, that is not a deliberate action on your part, so don't be concerned. Just concentrate more to keep a firm grip so you will not lose control. Remember, there is nothing more beautiful than a perfect swing and follow-through with both hands on the bat and your body in perfect position. Don't spoil that picture with a flying hand that gets you into trouble.

The Wrist Snap

There are many who claim that strong wrist action is the key to being a good hitter. I don't agree totally with that idea, but I certainly do suggest that all hitters work to strengthen their wrists. Strong wrist action (and forearms) will allow you to wait until the last possible second and still get after a pitch with some power, provided you get the bat moving as quickly as possible. Strong wrists will prevent you from being fooled because you can get after the pitch the instant you recognize what it really is. I'll always remember my teammate Rod Carew hitting against left-handers who had wicked sliders. He'd get way down and then snap off a line drive with a quick flick of his powerful wrists when others who did not possess that strength would get tied up.

I know that Hall of Famer Hank Aaron was renowned for his great wrist action, but what that meant was that he was able to wait just a microsecond longer before swinging. He was fooled less often than many other hitters, and the strength and speed from those wrists just pumped out home run after home run. His record 755 lifetime homers are testimony to what he did.

This is why we talked earlier in the book about beginning to do exercises that will strengthen your wrists. If you start a program and stay with it, I'll guarantee that within three or four weeks you'll notice a difference. The key then is to keep the strength program going for as long as you play.

Remember, what you do is in your hands.

VII. Arms & Shoulders: Two Key Hitting Tools

Just as the arms and shoulders are connected with the body, they are connected in their important role as key tools for hitting a baseball.

Use Every Inch of Your Arms

The key to good arm use is, quite simply, to use every inch from shoulder to wrist whenever you swing the bat. Don't be lazy. Extend those arms to the fullest and don't give it a how-do-you-do type of motion because that won't get you any kind of hitting consistency and...and even fewer base hits.

Every time you fully extend your arms when you swing, you have a better chance of hitting the ball hard, and full arm extension is particularly important when you pull the ball. Knowing that every time you hit the ball hard your chances for a hit also increase, I can't think of a better reason to concentrate on full arm extension with every bat swing.

Now that you know why the arms are important, it would be very easy to end our discussion. But let's take this a few steps further and look at what fully extended arms will do to other elements of your hitting talent.

The elbows will be locked when the arms are fully extended. To prove the point, grab an imaginary bat and hold your arms straight out in front of your body. What do you see? Your elbows are locked straight, not angled down slightly. Now, swing the bat with the arms straight out. Notice that at the same time that your elbows are in good position, your follow-through is also easy to complete. Your arms are not locked near your body, they go around in a nice, smooth, easy motion as you swing the bat. This gives you a quick, compact swing that can produce solid contact on the ball and the power you are looking for.

Believe me, you can only hit the ball hard when your arms are fully extended at impact. And if you want to pull the ball it's a necessity.

EXTEND THE ARMS: Arms fully extended during the swing will lock the elbows in a straight—and powerful—impact position, photo 7-1, 7-2.

Keep in mind, though, that even if you look to go to the opposite field with the ball, you must also have full arm extension to help guide the bat.

Arm extension is often a problem area because it's hard to know if you are achieving it. Every batter believes that when he is hitting the ball hard his arms are fully extended but someone else watching can quickly notice a halfway arm extension. Ask your coach to watch whenever you take batting practice to be certain that you are not falling into lazy habits. Waiting until a game can often be too late.

You may be wondering where to position your arms before you extend them. Because they tend to focus on the swing itself, young hitters often completely forget about this aspect of hitting. When you prepare to bat, make sure that your rear elbow is at least as high as your front elbow, and that its position makes an approximate forty-five-degree angle with the shoulder. Do not allow either elbow to be higher than your hands or your shoulders. Be sure not to pull them in too tight to your body, but don't worry too much about this. If your hands are about four to six inches away from your chest, as we discussed earlier in the book, your elbows will assume a natural and

ELBOW POSITION: Before swinging the bat, the rear elbow should be at least as high as the front elbow, photo 7-3, and in an approximate 45-degree angle to the shoulder. Neither elbow should be higher than the hands or shoulders; they should be held about 4 to 6 inches from the body.

comfortable distance away from the body. All of this will eventually produce a quicker swing and an easier follow-through with your bat, and when you swing you will be better able to meet the ball in front of you.

I realize that some hitters simply may be more comfortable with their elbows higher or lower than I have advised. But from nearly three decades of experience in the major leagues as player and coach, let me say that the most productive hitters always have positioned their elbows in the middle of the range.

One notable exception, however, is new Hall of Famer Carl Yastremski, who played so brilliantly for the Boston Red Sox for over two decades. For nearly three-quarters of his career he held his rear arm elbow up high, and during those years he was a marvelously productive hitter. When he got older and began experimenting with new stances every season, he lowered this elbow as he sought to compensate for his age and declining bat speed.

I am often asked why I am so adamant about getting those elbows in the middle, and I have a very simple answer. This keeps the head and eyes closer to the strike zone and makes it easier to see and hit the ball. If you raise your elbows, then you tend to stand more upright, thus raising the eye level and how you see the ball. Further, your arms would then have to make a major move downward to hit lower pitches, and that creates a longer, slower swing. Pitchers are trained to throw most of their pitches to the lower portion of the strike zone, so you're giving them an edge when you hold your elbows high. In like manner, if your elbows are too low, you have to bring them up to make a proper swing. In either case, it involves one more movement a hitter must make within the split second allotted to swing the bat. I always believed in eliminating those moves and using that split second to decide whether to swing and how to swing.

Hitters who can do this with elbows high or low in the ready position and be consistently productive should not change, or they will spoil a good thing. But if a hitter is not productive, even if he feels comfortable with his elbows high or low, then he *must* change and suffer all of the discomfort that goes with finding a new posture. The bottom line is not comfort but productivity.

I know the problem of faulty elbows—elbows held too high or too low at the ready position—often is not easy to detect. In most cases, hitters aren't even aware of it unless someone points it out. The key, of course, is to get into good habits and stay there. In that regard, try the following: In batting practice, stand farther away from the plate than normal. That will force you to extend your arms and keep everything in place, including locked elbows at impact, as you meet the ball.

To forestall any problems, it is not a bad idea to make that batting practice routine part of your daily hitting life and do it regardless of where you get the ball. Force those arms out and get in the habit of extending them. Remember, in a game you will be called upon either to hit the ball to the opposite field or to pull it, and you'll have to do it regardless of where the ball is pitched.

Thus, with a man on first base, if the manager flashes you a sign to hit the ball into the hole between first and second base, you must go get the pitch. If you want to execute the play properly, then all of your fundamentals had better be in order. That means extending those arms and elbows to make contact with that ball and get it behind the runner, if possible.

Once more, mastering the fundamentals will help you get the job done. Make a little game of batting practice by simulating those signs when you are hitting to the opposite field or pulling the ball. Get used to having to do the job as it is laid down for you.

Strengthen Those Arms

Extending the arms is one thing; but having the proper strength to fully utilize that good extension is also very necessary. Here is one area where every hitter should enter into a strength program of some kind and stay with it for as long as he plays baseball.

Don't get me wrong, because as I noted earlier in this book, I'm not asking baseball players to become weightlifters or put the same emphasis on strength as football players, but baseball players should take great care in making their arms—particularly the area from the wrist to the elbow—as strong as possible.

It doesn't take a lot of work, perhaps no more than ten to fifteen minutes a day with a program specifically designed for this one area. Chapter II gives some good examples of exercises. Some major leaguers spend three or four hours in a gym working on machines and other exercise routines when they could put that time to better use by taking extra hitting or working on pitching fundamentals. I never did much exercise for my upper body because I wanted to keep it loose and supple, but I always took care to work on my arms and wrist strength, and it paid off.

Let me say one final word on exercise and baseball: a make-sense general exercise program will not hurt your baseball skills. On the contrary, it will make you feel better and stronger all around, and if you do it year-round, you will be as ready to play when the spring rolls around as you are in mid-season. Make it a part of your routine.

Better Batting from the Shoulders Up

The shoulders play a big role in hitting. The worst thing a hitter can do is to dip his rear shoulder too much and drop his hands. The elbows drop with them, and the front shoulder flies out too soon. There goes your good hitting motion.

Like the arms, the shoulders are a part of that necessary hip and hand combination because all three work together. You simply cannot turn good shoulder position off and on. Get them set consistently and stay with them.

If you find your shoulders are not correctly in position, you might move your hands away from your body a bit and then force yourself to hit down on the ball to get a line drive or a sharp ground ball. This will get your shoulders acting together and get them even and on kilter as you stride into the ball.

However, the shoulders do not remain even throughout the swing. Try to keep them level—or even moving slightly downward—until you plant your front foot. Then drive the front shoulder up and out and the back shoulder down and through the hitting zone until it replaces the position of the front shoulder. This is very similar to the way a good golf swing is executed: the back shoulder working down and through the hitting or impact area.

It may take a keen-eyed coach or teammate to point out the problem if you haven't already sensed some trouble with dropping bat production. As soon as you become aware of it, get after the cure, or this can drag you into a deep hole that will be very hard to overcome.

I always believed in dipping my front shoulder—the one closest to the pitcher—just a bit because it kept my hips from opening too soon and thus pulling out my front shoulder too soon. This gets a bit tricky because as soon as I say, "Drop your front shoulder a bit," there is the danger of young hitters making too deep a bend and throwing off their stride and swing. Here is what you should do: Concentrate on looking down while still seeing the pitcher so you can pick up the ball as it leaves his hand. That sounds like doing two things at the same time that are impossible, but your vision can focus downward and still pick up the pitcher's hand. By looking down, you automatically lower your front shoulder a bit without disturbing the rest of your stance.

One last word of caution: Don't think constantly about your shoulders being down so much that you overlook something else. As I noted earlier, there is so much involved in hitting a baseball that you cannot afford to concentrate on just one thing. The reason I urge you to practice as much as possible is to ensure that all of this will become so natural that you'll only have to concentrate on hitting the baseball. I want you to practice away from the game, when you have time to get into a good groove, making sure your mechanics are perfect. Remember, you will play like you practice; if you have everything in order away from the game, then you will have everything in order during it.

VIII. The Swing Is The Thing

As the old hit tune from the forties noted, "It don't mean a thing if you ain't got that swing."

It may be a bit ungrammatical, but there never was a truer message ever given to any hitter. Yet there are as many different swings as there are hitters. It's not how you look, but what you do, and some guys can have an awful-looking swing and still be successful with it.

I know that a lot of young players try to develop their swing after their favorite player's style. I've often been asked if I ever patterned myself after anyone, and in looking back, I have to say, "Not exactly. I took bits and pieces from a lot of people."

When I came from Cuba, I had a wide open stance with a big swing. Later I shortened up a bit and cut down my swing. At all times, however, I kept myself in control and had good vision to pick up the ball when it left the pitcher's hand.

I also took great pride in my hitting and my ability to take a pitch and slap it to the opposite field. The fact that I could handle left-handed pitchers was a source of pride to me as a left-handed hitter. I got a bigger kick out of hitting a home run off a lefty than off a right-hander.

Even though I knew how and where to hit the ball, I learned a lot from playing with and against some great hitters like Rod Carew, Harmon Killebrew, Bobby Allison, Cesar Tovar, and Frank Robinson. I watched them and applied some of the practical things to my own game. Zoilo Versalles was another guy whose style was an inspiration. He was a skinny little guy who hit .270 and a bunch of home runs, and he had great technique and style.

And that's what it takes . . . work, work, work, which means practice, practice, practice. I can look around the American League now and easily spot the players who have worked hard to perfect their game, and the first place it shows is in how they swing the bat. None of them do it precisely the same, but all have picturesque swings in their own right.

Jose Canseco of the Oakland A's may have the most beautiful swing in the league right now, and his teammate Mark McGwire is not too far behind. Canseco's is hard but flat, level at every point he

HANDS, ELBOWS, AND SHOULDERS: *Kirby Puckett positions and moves his hands, elbows and shoulders as efficiently as possible in these photos. His hands and elbows are held a comfortable distance from his body, not too high, too low, or too close. When he begins his swing he moves his hands slightly closer to his body and slightly up (Photos 8-1B through 8-1G). This is a secret that Hall of Famer Ted Williams discovered when he played and has taught for years.*

DOWN AND THROUGH THE BALL: *Photos 8-1H through 8-1N show Kirby moving slightly down and through the ball. The back shoulder drives down and through as the left shoulder is pulled up and out by the opening of the hips. Kirby shows excellent discipline of the head, as it has dropped into the hitting area, thus keeping his eyes fixed on the ball (Photos 8-1M and 8-1N)*

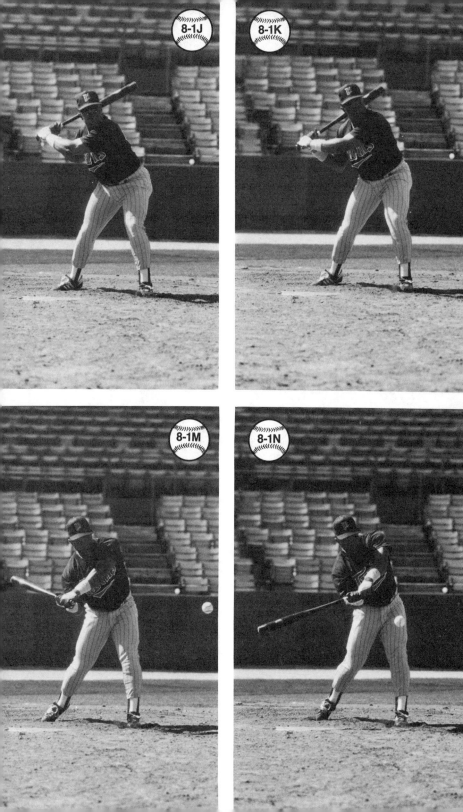

FULL EXTENSION AND LOCKED ELBOWS: *Like a properly executed golf swing, the baseball swing calls for full extension for maximum power. Greater power is the result of greater bat speed. And bat speed is produced by the rapid opening of the hips, thus pulling the front side open and the right side down and through the swing. The top hand guides the bat and accelerates it into the ball. Photos 8-10 and 8-1P show the results of a "quick hip" and strong top-hand and action—a powerful extension, with locked elbows, of the arms and a hard-hit ball coming off the bat.*

attacks the ball, which enables him to get into a pitch with great power and just crush it. McGwire has a big swing, and like many great sluggers, it is almost as exciting to watch him miss a pitch as it is to see him hit a homer.

Don Mattingly of the Yankees and George Brett of the Kansas City Royals are two other examples of great hitters with different swings . . . different yet still beautiful. Both of them wait on the ball, yet Mattingly has a more classic swing than Brett, who was a disciple of the late Charley Lau, a fine batting coach whose pupils all have a distinctive way of going after the ball. Gary Gaetti of the Twins is another who waits well on his pitch, and when he gets it, he doesn't miss with a compact swing that is just a blur.

Kirby Puckett, another Twin, is different. He does not have what you would call a *consistent* swing but he hits everything hard. He has good eyes and waits very well on a pitch. He will hit the ball hard about ninety percent of the time. Fred McGriff, the young first baseman of the Toronto Blue Jays, has one of the most perfect swings of any American League player. In fact, I never recall him taking a bad swing, and the amazing thing to me is that he has been in the majors for just a couple of years and he's already perfected the way he swings the bat.

Of course, I can't discuss swings without mentioning Wade Boggs of the Red Sox, who has the most beautiful inside-out swing in baseball. Whenever we're playing in Boston, I usually go out to Fenway Park early, and it is a marvel just to watch him work so diligently before practice. I guess I have a soft spot for him because so much of his work is centered around trying to hit line drive after line drive to left field—the opposite field for him as a left-handed hitter. You see the result of that work and that beautiful inside-out swing during a game when pitchers come inside on him and he still slaps the ball to the opposite field. The amazing thing is that because he is such a great hitter Wade could hit twenty home runs and still hit .350 every year, but he disdains the long ball and works to rack up his string of 200-hit seasons.

Make it S-M-O-O-O-T-H

What is a good swing? It all depends on you. It must be easy for you and it must make you productive. It is something you develop through constant practice, but it's not one that is aimed only at hitting home runs. If you aim for home runs, you'll probably lead your league in pop flies.

It is best to develop a line drive type of swing, because then you'll hit those long fly balls that go out of the ballpark. You'll also hit hard ground balls that will skip into the outfield or line drives that will find their way into power alleys. It's a lot easier to hit line drives than it is to hit fly balls . . . and a lot more satisfying, too.

I hear people say that hitters must develop a dead level swing, but there is no such thing as a dead level swing, if only because nineteen out of twenty pitches are never going to be in a location where you can swing the bat that way. I want hitters to develop a smooth swing that will enable them to hit the ball where it is pitched. Young hitters often think there is something wrong—or they cannot go after a pitch—unless the ball is right out in front where their bat will come across in a perfect arc.

Instead, hitters should concentrate on keeping their head level as they track the ball and then keeping the bat level as they swing, be it reaching up or down for the pitch. At all times, that swing is smooth, and if it is smooth, then the batter's worries about how level it is will disappear. That also means that if the ball is up and the hitter wants it, he should remember to swing down so that he will hit either a line drive or a hard grounder.

The best way to develop a good, smooth swing is to work on the following:

1. Concentrate on how you swing the bat.

2. Practice, practice, practice. You should take every chance you get to hit, to learn to pull the ball as well as to hit it to the opposite field. When you do, think line drive, and you will develop a line drive swing, which will help you to consistently hit the ball hard.

3. Away from the field, stand in front of a full-length mirror and, provided there is room, swing the bat as hard as you can. (Except, don't do it in your parents' bedroom and then blame me when everything goes flying!) You will get a good idea of what your swing looks like, how the bat looks going around, and how you look finishing your swing. I did that and would pretend the ball was just a few feet away as I began my swinging motion. If you do it enough and get a good picture of exactly what your swing is like, when you go to the park to hit, it will feel natural.

Hitters also must be aware of the glitches that can throw off a good swing:

1. Moving or lifting your head. Then the eyes can't watch the ball all the way, making it very hard to hit the ball.

2. Getting into bad habits and staying with them, either because no one picks them up or you refuse to change.

3. Jumping at the ball, by which the hitter opens his hips and brings

STANCE AND START: *Here's the swing from stance to stepping into the ball. Kirby Puckett sets up with his feet slightly wider than his shoulders, hands and lead-arm elbow held comfortably away from the body. He stands square in the box with his feet parallel, front foot closed. Photos 8-2D through 8-2G show the "quiet foot" movement when striding into the ball. Notice how Kirby has moved slightly down and into the pitch. This keeps his front shoulder closed until committing to swing, and his head and eyes in good position to follow the pitch.*

WEIGHT TRANSFER: *Photos 8-2H through 8-2N depict the flow of Kirby's weight from his back leg to the front leg and the quick action of his hips. Once the front foot is planted, the hips open and the front shoulder is pulled out and up to allow the right shoulder and hands direct access to the hitting area. Like the golf swing, the correct movement through the hitting area, especially on low pitches, calls for the right shoulder to drive down, through and—after contact—up.*

CONTACT: *Photos 8-2O through 8-2U show the front foot still slightly closed as the weight is rolled over to a firm, or rigid front leg. This front foot finally opens when the hip-turn is complete (Photos 8-2R through*

8-2Q

8-2U). *Notice the full extension that Kirby achieves as his bat meets the ball (Photos 8-2Q and 8-2R), and that the ball has been met in front of the plate.*

FOLLOW-THROUGH: *Notice that Kirby's top hand does not leave the bat until the swing is complete and the ball has been met (Photos 8-2U through 8-2X). Kirby's head stays down, his eyes focused on the ball, until well after the ball has left the bat. The head does not come up until the ball is sighted off the bat (Photo 8-2V).*

his hands forward too soon. This produces what amounts to a punchless half swing, and about all you can expect from that is a weak ground ball or an easy fly ball.

Don't Change Your Swing, Move Your Feet

One of the biggest mistakes a hitter can make is adjusting his swing every time he adjusts his position in the batter's box. It's okay to move your hands up or down a bit, but if you're going to change anything, make it the way you position your feet, not the way to swing the bat. In fact, once you develop a swing that suits you and feels comfortable, don't ever change it—and don't let anyone talk you into changing it unless they detect a serious flaw. And even then, if you are producing, how serious can any flaw be?

I know it may get to sound like a broken record (or is it a compact disc now?), but learn to use your bat to hit to all fields. You can do this by changing your position in the batter's box, not altering the swing, and still take on any pitcher. If you begin to make a lot of changes, you'll lose consistency and get into trouble. You want to give your hands an opportunity to work and to swing the bat, so it is easier to move your feet.

Here are some keys:

1. If you're hitting to the opposite field, move away from the plate, slightly close your stance, and get more of an angle on where you wish to hit. All the pitches will be away from you, that means you give the plate to the pitcher, but you'll get the plate back when you stride into the pitch. Don't worry about losing any power because a good, hard swing will send that ball flying.

2. If you want to pull the ball, put your back foot closer to the plate. Assume an open or square stance, whichever is more comfortable. You will get a better look at the pitcher's delivery, from when he takes the ball into his hand until he releases it. Be quick with your bat, but remember—don't move your hands or change your swing. The change in your foot position is all you need.

3. If you're facing a pitcher who has a mediocre breaking ball, move to the front of the batter's box and with a good hard swing, get the ball before it breaks. The pitcher will nibble you to death if you give him the plate, so get up on it.

4. If you face a tough breaking ball pitcher, move back in the box where you'll get a longer look at the ball and its movement.

5. If you want to hit a fly ball, concentrate on getting a pitch you can lift. In general you have a better chance to hit a fly ball than a

grounder, but if you come to bat with less than two out and a runner on third base during the first four innings of a game, you have to make sure you don't hit it on the ground to third base. By getting a bit of an uppercut on your swing, you should be able to lift the ball without disrupting the smoothness.

6. If you have a hit-and-run situation, you'll want the ball on the ground. Get on top of it when you swing and hit in a slight downward motion.

The Quick Bat

A hitter who can hit a pitcher's best pitch, like a hard slider on the corner of the plate, because he can wait till the last second before swinging, is said to have a "quick bat." I worked to get one myself, and I helped accomplish this by opening my feet, not by making a major change in my swing.

Just remember a quick bat is not only quick hands; it is quick hips and quick hands. The hands follow in the sequence of the swing motions, so keep them back and then let them fly once your weight goes over to the front foot and the hips start opening. The hands must move as quickly as possible once the hips begin pulling your shoulders, arms and hands through the swing. Here is something to avoid: transferring your weight to the front foot and then trying to determine if you're going to swing. It won't work. Once your weight transfers to the front foot, you must explode into the ball.

Let me say, too, that quickness with the bat is often as much a state of mind as it is a state of swing. There will be times when a hitter does not feel quick, but he must make up his mind that he has to be. For instance, if Roger Clemens of the Red Sox, a ninety-mile-per-hour pitcher, is pitching, there is little chance you will get a ball you can pull. So you must be ready and do what you can with the pitch you get. The best way is to go with the pitch, regardless of what is thrown. Tell yourself that you are quick, wait as long as possible with your hands back, and then go after that ball.

All of which brings me back to some key points. When you know the pitcher is tough on you, give him the plate and go to the opposite field by striding into the ball. When you stride into the ball, you get the plate back. You will make it easier to hit because all the balls will be away from you.

IX. Bunting: It Need Not Be A Lost Art

Too often I hear baseball people complain that bunting has become a lost art. I hope not because no hitter can really afford to be without it. However, many young players look at the sluggers in the game and think that's where all the prestige and money is going to be; unfortunately, they are not too wrong.

"But," I say to them, "how many of you are going to hit 40 home runs every year? How many of you are going to drive in 130 runs a year?"

The reply is usually silence, or at best, as more-hopeful-than-realistic, "Maybe some day I will . . ."

"Maybe some day you will . . . and maybe some day you never will," I tell them. "So you had better be prepared to find other ways to get your hits and the popularity that good hitters can enjoy."

Then I tell them about my former Twins' roommate, Rod Carew, who sometimes added thirty-five hits a year to his total because he was such a great bunter. I want them to understand that they can do the same thing, maybe add twenty or thirty hits a year to their total if they learn how to bunt.

"Do you realize what twenty or thirty hits a yet can do to a batting average?" I ask them. "It can make a .270 hitter a .300 hitter, and it can make a .230 hitter a .270 hitter. Thirty hits a year represents about one-fifth of the total for most major league hitters."

I don't know of any better incentive for finding another way to build your batting average, whether you are a major league player or not.

Carew made a believer out of me, although maybe too late because I was never much of a bunter. After watching him, I became convinced of what it can do for a hitter apart from sacrifice and squeeze play situations.

The first time he impressed me was in his rookie year when we played the Baltimore Orioles, who had the great Brooks Robinson playing third base. "I'm going to bunt on him," Rod told me.

"Roomie," I said, trying to be patient with this rookie who obviously didn't know who Robinson was and what he could do around the bag, "he's the best in the business. Don't try to bunt on him."

"If I do it right," he replied, "he won't throw me out."

And he was right! In his first at bat, he laid down a perfect bunt and beat it out. And he kept that up for the rest of a career that will ultimately land him in the Hall of Fame.

He did it against all third basemen, regardless of reputation. One day against the Oakland A's, which had Sal Bando at third base, he got three bunt hits—and Bando was playing him halfway down the line!

But there is also a lesson in Carew's skills. He worked as hard at bunting as he did at hitting, and he finished his career with a .330 average. Some days in spring training, he would practice bunting thirty-five minutes at a stretch. Often, he went to the park for extra hitting and spent the entire time working on his bunting skills . . . all of which made him one of the greatest bunters in the game's history.

Some might say, "Fine, but maybe that was all he could do." I just laugh because there wasn't a pitcher or a pitch that Rod Carew couldn't handle, in any situation. He just used his bunting to give him one more weapon and open up more holes in the infield. First, second, and third basemen simply could not afford to play at normal depth when he came to bat. As I noted, also, his .330 lifetime average is ample testimony to his ability to hit.

It Starts with the Mind

Becoming an effective bunter is as much a mental skill as it is physical. Many players, and this includes major leaguers, simply don't like to bunt and they don't work at it. Sometimes when they take batting practice, they'll bunt the first pitch, and if it goes foul, they just shrug their shoulders and say, "So what. I'm a good bunter when I have to be," and they go on to hitting. You can't do that. Hitters must keep after it until they get it right. One good bunt can win a game, and the failure of one player to bunt at the right time can lose a game. How many times have you seen that happen?

Bunting also usually means giving yourself up in sacrifice situations, and there are many selfish players who simply don't want to do that. I've seen many instances where a manager flashes the bunt sign to a batter, with a man on base, and the batter simply takes the pitch. He gets it again, and again he takes the pitch, often for strike two, putting him in a big hole against the pitcher. That is his way of telling the manager he doesn't want to do this.

Of course, I've seen managers—and I've done it myself during my managing stints in the minor leagues and in Latin America—who will flash that bunt sign a third time as a warning that "I know what you're trying to do and I won't tolerate it." And here, I'm talking mainly about players who know how to bunt but simply refuse to make the effort.

SACRIFICE POSITION: *Tony Oliva has begun to move and face the pitcher while also sliding his hand up the bat to a point just below or at the trademark, photo 9-1A. His bat is held so that it fully covers the plate and his body is squared up to the pitcher, photo 9-1B. He also holds his bat with his fingers slightly open and at a slightly raised angle to the ground, being sure that the bat is in front of the plate, photo 9-1C.*

DOWN THE LINE: *Tony lays a sacrifice down the base line but positions his body and his bat so the ball will land as close to the line as possible, photos 9-3A, 9-3B, 9-3C He draws back the bat slightly to cushion the impact of the ball and forces it to the ground, photos 9-3D, 9-3E.*

I've also seen times where players getting the bunt sign deliberately foul off the first two pitches, figuring they can then hit away. And I've seen managers—including myself—who will flash that bunt sign a third time, knowing full well that the hitter will make contact, because if he has another fouled bunt attempt he will be out on strikes.

Let me give it to you straight: Every hitter called upon to sacrifice must be willling to carry out the play. Sacrifice is just that—a willingness to give up one's chance for a hit for the good of the team in a certain situation. The more players a team has with that attitude, the more successful it will be. Do you know something else? It is no secret when situations call for bunts. Everyone in the park knows it, so it should be no big deal for any batter.

While everyone in the ballpark may know that a bunt is the obvious play, it still can be somewhat mysterious because the opposition doesn't know precisely when it will happen. The rule, then, is not to give yourself up right away or at least don't telegraph the move. Often you see poor bunters set themselves in the bunting position before the pitcher even releases the ball, and sure enough, here come the first and third basemen sitting right on top of him so they can make a play and get the base runner.

It is best to wait until after the pitcher has released the ball, and then turn your body halfway—some who are not good bunters go full-

BUNTING FOR A HIT TO FIRST:
Tony holds his bat the same way as if he were going to sacrifice, photos 9-4A, 9-4B, but instead of drawing back the bat to cushion the ball's impact, he pushes it forward beyond the plate, photo 9-4C as he takes off for first base.

BUNTING FOR A HIT TO THIRD:
Tony, as a left-handed batter, must take more care to push the ball into fair territory near the line so he cannot begin to run until the ball strikes the bat, photos 9-5A, 9-5B, 9-5C. To get good contact he will try to bunt a low strike and hold the bat at a slight downward angle.

face, but I don't advocate that. Polish the skill so you can do a half turn in the batter's box, because that also gives you the ability to swing away and slap the ball past an onrushing fielder. I did that many times, and I had enough power that if they got hit with the ball, it hurt!

Everyone doesn't bunt the same way because you see some players who walk up in the batter's box to get the ball, others who just move their feet while maintaining their basic stance, and still others who do that 45-degree turn and give themselves good position.

Position of the Bat

There are different ways to bunt depending on what you want to do with the ball. However, some things are the same for all bunts. The bat must be in front of the plate when it strikes the ball. If not, the chances are the ball will go foul or straight back to the pitcher who can get an easy play and take away any chance you might have to leg out an infield hit.

Have the barrel of the bat raised slightly, with not too much of a firm grip. Hold the bat by the fingertips, with the hands toward the middle of the bat. Above all, don't hold the top hand too tightly because a looser grip will absorb the ball striking the bat and cause the ball to die or slow down quicker once it hits the ground. If the bat is held firmly, the ball will ricochet off the bat and get to the fielder much more quickly.

At the same time, bring the hands and bat back a bit to further cushion the ball striking the wood, and then lastly, guide the bat so the ball will go toward either first or third base.

Here are the different ways to hold the bat depending on what you want to do with the bunt:

1. *Sacrifice*. Move your hand halfway up the bat, close to the barrel, with the fingers a little open. Don't go too far up the barrel lets your fingers get hit by the ball. Hold it loosely so the ball will go down and lose momentum as it hits the ground.

2. *Base hit*. The bat should be held the same way, with care taken not to tighten the grip. But instead of drawing back on the bat when striking the ball, the bat must be pushed forward a bit because the hitter—particularly a left-handed hitter—usually has begun his move toward first base when he goes after the ball. The batter must make certain that he gets the bat in front of the plate. Right-handed hitters must wait longer before committing to bunt, until the ball is almost to

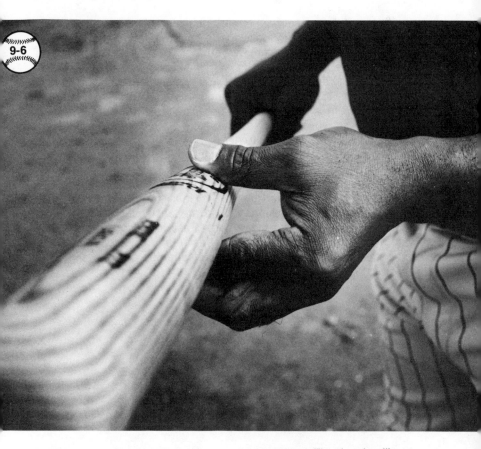

9-6

HAND POSITION: *The lower hand holds the bat securely and the top hand slides upward so only the fingertips will grasp it lightly near the trademark The thumb will rest atop the trademark, slightly behind the surface of the bat that will strike the pitched ball, photo 9-6.*

the plate while lefties can reach out sooner and get a quicker start. I always believe third base is a good spot for lefties to get this kind of bunt because the fielder is playing back and must make a longer throw after he fields it.

3. *Squeeze.* The emphasis here is just making contact with the ball, but the bat still should be held in a loose manner so the ball will lose momentum when it hits the ground. Just make certain the ball hits the bat.

Control of the bat is most important. Be careful of that loose grip, because it cannot be so loose that a pitch will knock the bat out of your hands. You should not throw your bat at a ball, as you often hear is the case, because you lessen your chances of making any contact at all. The only time I ever did that was when I was fooled by a pitch, and I had already made up my mind to bunt regardless of what the pitcher threw.

Carew was different in this respect. He could draw his bat back and take the pitch if it wasn't to his liking. But that came from practice and a mastery of this delicate art. Practice, regardless of the level of competition, is so important and should be done on a continuous basis. Bunters have to handle all kinds of pitches, and in definite bunting situations, a hitter can expect that the pitcher will not give him anything easy. Breaking pitches are easier than fastballs because the hitter can get a better look. Fastballs also hit the bat and carom off with more force, making it easier for the fielder. At any rate, the batter must be able to hit any pitch when he gets the sign for a bunt.

X. Building A Book On The Pitcher

You hear a lot about major league hitters having a "book" on opposing pitchers. This means that teams keep a detailed catalog of all the opposing pitchers and what they can do in all situations—the pitches they throw best and the ones which are easiest to hit. Before every game, the hitting coach will remind his players of what to expect.

Of course, pitchers also keep a book on the hitters as well, and before every game, the pitching coach and catcher have a pre-warmup meeting in which they review strengths and weaknesses. In each case, the "book" is updated almost weekly as advance scouts see opposing teams and note any changes.

When scouting hitters, the key is whether or not they are in a slump or on a hot streak, what pitches they are creaming, and what pitches are giving them problems. Scouts of pitchers look for those who have lost control of breaking pitches and may have to rely on mediocre fastballs, or those who have developed a new pitch and whether or not it's been effective. They look at how the bullpen is producing and who may be overworked or slowed by injuries or fatigue. In short, there are many delicious tidbits of information that hitters and pitchers eagerly devour so they can get an edge on their opposition.

Individual players don't just wait for teams to do this, because every hitter and pitcher has his own "book" on the opposition that is based on personal experience. As a hitter, I knew what to expect from every pitcher I ever faced if I had played against him in the past. I knew his best pitches and the ones I could handle better, and I knew what he liked to do in certain situations, such as when he had me at 0-and-2 or 1-and-2. What the club scouting report gave me were things I would have no way of knowing, such as an injury or the fact that in recent games he may have been struggling with certain pitches. Those I built into my own game plan along with the information in my "book."

The point here is that you don't have to be a major league hitter to get a "book" on the pitcher. Young hitters who play baseball in their communities will encounter the same pitchers time and again. Every time you face that pitcher, you should be making mental notes. Some farsighted hitters keep real books, usually a small notebook that they can stuff into their pockets and update what that pitcher does after every at-bat. There certainly is nothing wrong with this approach because it provides a fresh reference after every at bat, and is a handy guide that leaves no margin for the errors that sometimes occur when a player tries to remember what happened several weeks or a month ago.

The Book's Table of Contents

What sort of information should go into your "book" on opposing pitchers? Here is a good list:

1. *Delivery.* Watch the pitcher warm up for fifteen or twenty minutes, particularly if you haven't faced him before. Watch his pitches and how they are moving, and if you have faced him before, get an idea if he's changed at all. See how he throws various pitches. Do his fastballs come from an overhand delivery or are they three-quarter sidearm? How are his breaking balls moving, and what sort of delivery does he use for them? All of this can help you directly in the game.

It has worked for me many times, such as in the 1965 World Series against the Dodgers. Sandy Koufax, the Dodgers' Hall of Fame left-handed pitcher, was scheduled to pitch in the second game of the Series, and I had never faced him before. I watched him warm up before the game and got a good idea of how he threw his great fastball and curve. In the sixth inning of a scoreless game, I doubled against him to drive in the first run and help to open the gates to a 5-1 victory. Without that "extra peek" before the game, I don't know whether I could have handled him like that.

2. *Pitch release.* Many pitchers have two different types of deliveries for their pitches, and you must know them both to have a better chance to hit the pitches. A pitcher may release his fastball from one spot and his breaking pitch from another. He may easily tip that off during his warmup, or if you have faced him in the past, then you should also have a good idea. If you can spot those release points as he is delivering the ball, then you'll have a solid idea of what kind of pitch is coming.

Let me say here that I'm amazed at how many pitchers, even at the major league level, signal their pitches because they have not learned to deliver every ball with the same motion from the same spot. For example, they deliver their fastball from the top but drop down to throw the breaking pitch. Give a good hitter an inkling of that and he should be sitting on those pitches when he swings the bat. That, of course, comes from intense study by the hitter.

3. *Types of action.* What kind of movement should you look for in the fastball, sinker, and slider? The overhand fastball will be the number one pitch for a right- or left-handed pitcher if he can get anything on it, and you can look for speed rather than movement with this pitch. However, since the snap for the sinker or slider is different from the snap for the fastball, you can definitely expect some action with these pitches. A sinker ball is "turned over" a bit more by the way the pitcher holds the ball in his fingers and releases it. The slider is more difficult to pick up because it looks like a fastball on release, but if the pitcher cuts it enough, it will move away at the last minute. Good fastballs, on the other hand, often move up rather than away. A pitcher who has a good slider can be very effective if he has control because that is a very tough pitch to hit, but if a pitcher has a slow slider, it is easier to pick up because it will move more like a flat-breaking curveball and a batter can track it more easily.

4. *Pitching from the stretch.* The rules change here because the pitcher now has two concerns: the hitter and the base runner. He must throw the ball not only to get the hitter out but also to prevent the runner from getting a good jump toward the next base. So be on guard for a quicker move to the plate. Hitters will not get many slow-breaking balls because the pitcher doesn't want to give the runner an edge to steal a base. Also hitters should be looking for sinker balls because the pitcher will be trying to get a double-play ground ball to the infield. With no one on base, a hitter can be almost certain a pitcher will take more time in releasing the ball.

While it is important to have as much knowledge of a pitcher as possible, don't ever go into a game stuck in one mental rut. In other words, you sometimes must adjust to the pitcher and what he does or is forced to do.

Pitching Styles

Let's look at three types of pitchers:

1. *The Soft Thrower or "Junk" Pitcher.* This kind of pitcher has only one aim—to survive by keeping hitters off-stride and by surprising them. Tommy John, who had such a distinguished career with several major league teams for almost a quarter century, was the best example. Long after he lost a very good fastball, he succeeded better than anyone I ever saw with an array of off-speed pitches and the ability to hit corners and keep hitters off-stride.

Young players will probably not see many "junk" throwers, but every so often a clever guy comes along who pitches as much with his head and an array of junk as he does with his arm. In that instance, hitters should almost pretend they are playing slow-pitch softball; stay back, be very patient, and use the entire field. The only things in the body that should move quickly are the hands, to adjust for better bat control.

It takes a great deal of concentration and patience to deal with these tantalizing pitches. I've seen major league hitters totally lose their cool and begin yelling, "How did you get me out with those pitches!" The key is not to allow the pitcher to outsmart you and force you to go for pitches you don't want to hit. A lack of patience means swinging at pitches which will either be called "balls" by the umpire or, worse still, become dinky grounders. These kinds of pitchers are often death on pull hitters who become so anxious they fall into the junk trap. Don't give in—get that ball to the opposite field if necessary. If he makes a mistake and puts the ball in your wheelhouse, then tag it.

2. *The Wild Pitcher.* These pitchers are harder to hit than those who throw strikes. Again, patience is the key. Don't help them out by swinging at their wild pitches, because if left to their own devices, they'll be out of the game by the second inning with hits, walks, and wild pitches.

If your team is facing a wild pitcher, and he walks the batter ahead of you, make him pitch to you! Don't go after the first couple of pitches unless they are truly good, otherwise you just help him out of a jam. If you are patient, you may get a walk or a good pitch.

3. *The Good Fastball Pitcher.* Don't ever worry about being fooled or trying to be too patient. You won't have a chance. He's coming after you as a hitter, so you must go after him before he gets you in a hole. You become a defensive hitter.

Construct Your Hitting Game Plan

Before you ever step into the batter's box, you must have a good idea of what you want to do as a hitter. If you go to the plate with the intention of taking the first pitch, then do it, and do it even if you see the fattest watermelon in the world coming at you. You already have made up your mind to take the pitch, so even though your body may not want to do it, the back of your mind is still focused on taking the pitch. You never wind up swinging very well when you're trying to fight that battle.

Also, many hitters become more aggressive and confident after they take a pitch because a batter, I believe, simply isn't consistently mentally ready to hit the first pitch. He needs to take a look at what the pitcher does or to be challenged by that ball zinging past him, even if it isn't a strike. A good example is Wade Boggs. He invariably takes every first pitch because it builds up his confidence. You can look it up, and you'll find that Boggs is a better hitter after the first pitch because it focuses his attention.

Many times a pitcher will start a hitter off with a breaking ball, and most hitters simply aren't in a mental or physical groove to take on that kind of pitch right away. So hitters get fooled as much by the break of the ball as by their own mental inaction and indecision. Know what you want to do—and most importantly, what you don't want to do—and then stay with that original thought.

If you still are skeptical or need further convincing, consider that eighty percent of the times a hitter does hit the first pitch, he does not hit it very well. This is because he is not ready and has not begun to concentrate and bear down.

The first pitch isn't the only time you need to have a mental set. Sometimes I've heard guys who took a called third strike come back to the dugout and say, "Gee, he made a good pitch on me. I wouldn't have hit it anyway." That's just an excuse for being dumb. With two strikes, you should always swing at anything near the strike zone. For one thing, if you get a called strike three, then most of the time the pitch was good enough to swing at. And who knows, if you had swung at it, maybe you would have gotten a base hit.

Some players say they are choosy about what pitches they wish to hit, but often players get more hits on bad pitches than on good ones. A batter is at the plate by himself and can make the choice of what he wants to hit, but he should also have a good idea of the strike zone and be close enough to it so he can handle any pitches that get there. Also remember that it is difficult to swing at a third strike if you've already let the first two go past. So, it is okay to take the first pitch, but then you must be ready to hit the second pitch.

If you have a 3-0 count with a man on third base and two outs or less, and the manager flashes you the hit sign, then do it. Concentrate on that pitch—unless it is too far to reach—and go and get it. If you try to be careful and draw a walk on a pitch you can hit, the opposition now has set up a good double play situation, and that runner still is sitting on third base, in jeopardy of not getting home. If you had swung at the pitch, you probably would have gotten him home.

There are times when you can be fairly certain of the type of pitch that will be coming at you. You'll have an edge if you expect it. If you are ahead 2-0, look for a fastball because the pitcher doesn't want to get behind 3-0. If the count is 3-1, you can look for a breaking ball because the pitcher wants you to swing at something you will have a problem with or one that might result in an easier out. On 3-2, there is a good chance you will get a fastball. Don't let it go by. You'll look awful ugly taking a called third strike three on a fastball. The pitcher is trying to get you out on 3-2, and the fastball is usually most pitchers' bail-out throw.

Many pitchers, once they are at advanced levels, also are predictable in their pitching selection. Some will go with a fastball, then a breaking pitch, and back to a fastball. Others will throw two fastballs, then a breaking pitch, and back to a couple of fastballs. There are some who start inside, then go outside, and back inside on a regular basis. If you know a pitcher works in an unbroken pattern, then you can devise a plan of when and what you wish to hit. All of this comes with experience and concentration—most importantly, concentration —as you face the same pitchers time and again.

This is of top interest to major leaguers when they get to the World Series and know there are only a limited number of games. When we defeated the St. Louis Cardinals in the 1987 World Series, our scouts had prepared a book on the Cardinals pitching staff, similar in content to the areas that I covered earlier in this chapter. In capsule form, here is what was said about some of the Cardinals pitchers:

John Tudor—He is not overpowering and tries to get by with a combination of sliders, screwballs, change-ups, and a so-so fastball. It is best to go to the opposite field against him, unless he makes a mistake as he did against Don Baylor who nailed him for a big home run. However, when he is on, you can't wait until the ninth inning to attack because by that time it is usually too late. There comes a time in the middle innings when hitters must get aggressive and begin slapping those off-speed pitches to other fields.

Joaquin Andujar—He is a powerful pitcher who challenges hitters with a good fastball and curve and then can drop down to three-quarters speed for other breaking pitches to keep hitters off-stride. He is also a good-brush back pitcher and uses that weapon when he is ahead. Be ready for a fastball on the inside because he wants the entire plate.

Todd Worrell—This Cards reliever throws fastballs about ninety percent of the time, and they are in the ninety-miles-per-hour range. Hitters must be ready when they face him.

Bob Cox—He has a good breaking ball and fastball. His ball moves well, and he uses the fastball most of the time. He doesn't waste any pitches, so be ready for his best pitch at all times. He will also come after hitters on the inside.

Armed with those basic facts, as well as up-to-date information on just how those pitchers were doing at the time, our hitters did a good job. Of course, there are always some disbelievers, but one of the greatest lessons ever taught occurred in the 1975 World Series between the Red Sox and Cincinnati Reds when Tony Perez stroked a tie-making, two-run homer late in the seventh game off Red Sox left-hander Bill Lee. Friends on the Sox told me later that their scouting report said that under no circumstances should Perez be given a change-up pitch, and that was underlined in the written report. But Lee, who often went his own way and did what he wanted, decided to challenge Perez—and the report—and he and the Red Sox paid dearly by losing the Series in that seventh game.

But all of the help in the world, from all of the scouts, really won't help a hitter unless he is willing to help himself. He must mentally prepare himself whenever he steps into the batter's box, follow the advice which has been given to him, and then not try to outsmart either the pitcher or himself. In the end the only person he fools will be himself, and how smart is that?

XI. Think Sharply To Hit Well

There are components that I call "get in the game" factors, when a player must be aware at all times just what the situation may require when he goes to bat. Sure, a coach may remind him, but often it's too late when the player steps into the batter's box. Keen awareness requires that a player have his mind working on these situations when he is sitting on the bench, awaiting his turn at bat.

One major reason is that the game is played differently in the first four innings than it is in the last five . . . and those final five most often decide the outcome. In the first four innings, hitters are pretty much on their own, unless they are facing a very tough pitcher and the manager knows he may not get many runs. Then hitters can anticipate being called upon to bunt for sacrifices, hit to the opposite field, get a fly ball into the outfield for a sacrifice fly, or anything to produce a precious run or two.

Otherwise, the manager is apt to let the batter go after the pitcher and try to blow him away. If it works and his team is ahead by a comfortable margin, then everything pretty much stays the same for the rest of the game.

But, if the game is close going into the final five innings, the coach or manager will exercise much tighter control over his hitters. Hitters then must be aware of base runners and what they can do, who is hitting behind them in the order and what they can do, and the pitcher and what he is doing.

For example, if you're the eighth hitter and have some power but the ninth guy can't hit a lick, then you have to take matters into your own hands with runners on and try any way possible to get those men home or move them along the bases.

But if you're a leadoff or second hitter and have good hitters after you, you have to be very certain not to snuff out an existing rally, or crimp a potential one. Thus, if there is a runner on first base in a close or tied game, you must be thinking about moving that runner to second base. You must try to hit the ball to right field, on the ground. If a right-handed batter faces a tough pitcher, he knows he'll get inside pitches to prevent him from going to right field, with the added hope that he'll try to pull those balls into potential double play grounders. So the hitter must be disciplined and forget pulling those pitches; he should adjust his stance and try to poke them to the opposite field.

If you find that tough to do, why not lay down a bunt? I did that many times in such situations, and if I got a hit, then our rally continued; if I was out, most often I had moved the runner along and into scoring position.

Beware the Pitcher's Traps

As we noted in the preceding chapter, pitchers work differently according to the situation. With runners on first and second base, for instance, they will work to trick a hitter rather than try to mow him down. They are looking for that easy grounder that becomes a potential double play ball.

That is the time the hitters must take charge of themselves and not give in mentally to the pitcher. It may mean the hitter forcefully telling himself, "This is not the time I want to hit the ball on the ground. I want to hit a line drive or get the ball to the opposite field." Then the hitter will be into the game mentally and will have mapped out a game plan for that situation.

The next step is implementing it, and here knowledge of the pitcher is important. The hitter can be certain that he will get some kind of sinking pitch, in on his knuckles, to try and force the double play grounder. He shouldn't try to pull those pitches; he should go instead, as I just noted, to the opposite field by stepping back in the box. If the pitcher misses a couple of times inside, he has him 2-0, and the pitcher must come in with a strike. Now, the batter has the advantage and can look for a good pitch.

"But Doctor, I Just Can't Hit a Breaking Ball...And He Knows It"

I hear that a lot from hitters who are bugged by the prospect of taking on a breaking ball pitcher in key situations. My reply isn't always what hitters like to hear: You can't give up! Otherwise, you'll get nothing but a steady diet of breaking balls and then what are you going to do?

In fact, there are three things you should do:

1. If you have problems hitting breaking pitches, work as much as you can in extra hitting trying to solve your weakness.
2. You must make up your mind when you go to the plate that the pitcher is not going to get you out with a breaking pitch. Therefore,

concentration becomes a key, and you do anything possible not to let it happen.

3. Don't try to pull the ball (where have you heard that before?) but work to get the ball to the opposite field. Often when you try to pull a breaking pitch, you move your head and you don't follow the path of the ball from the pitcher's hand to the plate. Therefore, you must concentrate on not moving your head and following the ball, hitting it to the other field if necessary.

Knowing Your Limitations and Working with Them

If you know what your limitations are, then everything else is a strength, and you know the pitchers will avoid your strengths. Therefore, I recommend that you follow the Triple P plan:

1. Practice. Once you accept your limitations, then you can work to overcome them and to improve your strengths. For instance, shortly after I began playing pro ball, I became a good pull hitter. But it didn't take me long to realize that I had to learn how to use the entire field, and I wasn't really capable of doing that at that time. But I worked on it, and it later became one of my strengths.

2. Preparation. If the pitcher knows you have problems hitting an inside pitch, that's what you'll see, particularly in tough situations. So you have to mentally prepare yourself to handle those.

3. Patience. You need confidence in yourself, and that comes after you have given attention to points 1 and 2. You don't have to jump on the first couple of pitches. You can concentrate and tell yourself that by being patient you will get something you can handle, again even if it means giving yourself a little pep talk. Tell yourself, "I am the best. I can handle the pitch, and I want to be in this situation." Then give it your best shot. If you do it, fine; if you don't, maybe the guy behind you will. But at least, go up there with the idea of not giving in, of getting what you need and then going after it.

Getting Comfortable at Bat

The comfort I'm referring to has nothing to do with your stance but everything to do with your state of mind.

On a personal note, I had that comfortable feeling from the first moment I played professional baseball in the United States because I came here knowing I could hit the ball, no matter who was pitching.

Then I just wanted to get better, and I've explained how I learned to expand my hitting talent so that there never was a situation that I couldn't handle. As a young player, I was mostly a straight-away hitter, and many of my home runs went over the center field and right center field fence. Therefore, I worked on pulling the ball, and I mastered that art. Then when I saw that pitchers worked to take that away, I concentrated on going to the other field and worked hundreds of hours to perfect that talent.

It didn't stop there, either. I always reported to spring training in perfect physical condition, unlike many players of that time who came in ten or twenty pounds overweight and had the idea they would get themselves in shape during spring training and be ready when the season began. I played winter ball, even in my prime season in the late sixties and early seventies, because I felt I would be a better player in the major leagues. And after every season of winter ball, I had excellent major league seasons.

I never was completely satisfied with what I did, even in the final seasons of my career when I had pretty much mastered all of my hitting skills; I always felt I could do a little better. Rod Carew was the same way, and today, I see those traits in Kirby Puckett.

The result? Carew could do anything he wanted when it came to hitting the ball, Puckett is just about at the same point, and I was, too.

Breaking a Slump

If hitters are paying attention to their skills, they should never really get into slumps. Slumps don't come like bolts of lightning, fast and with no warning, but rather, a hitter can feel his timing begin to slip even before it reaches the point where he goes into a slump. As soon as a hitter senses, even slightly, that his timing is becoming faulty, he should get after the problem. He should get some extra hitting and check his swing and his stance.

If you feel yourself going into a slump, check all of the physical actions that are needed to hit. Look in the mirror while you swing and compare that to how you looked when things were going well. Then go out and get some hitting: ten to twenty minutes to the opposite field, fifteen to twenty minutes pulling the ball, fifteen to twenty minutes of general hitting.

I never believed in "sitting out" a slump, hoping it would go away with some rest and time off. Work is the key.

My old standby—hitting to the opposite field—is one way to cure a malady because you at least get confidence that the hits are there. This works because many mechanical problems—which you may not be aware of—can be solved by concentrating on this one idea. By trying to hit to the opposite field, you succeed unconsciously in keeping your front side closed longer, seeing the ball better, and keeping your hands back longer. Once you get a few hits, you feel better, and then you can begin to work on the other factors in your game. Sooner or later, maybe in three or four days, you have everything back in synch, and in the meantime neither your average nor your confidence has suffered too much.

When a "Slump" Isn't a Slump

I've seen hitters go into so-called "slumps" where they have hit the ball hard, but those balls just haven't fallen for hits. The player moans about being in a slump, and he gets depressed and loses his confidence.

Don't do that when you hit the ball well. Stay with it because if hitters really get into slumps, the first clue that they are solving their problems is good contact with the ball. I recall going into Baltimore to play the Orioles in 1969 in a kind of slump, and during a five-game series, I got seventeen hits in twenty-one at-bats. The year before in Boston, I was lagging along at about .250 near mid-season, and I got five hits in one game. Those five hits laid end to end really weren't equal to one good hit—an infield bleeder here, another there, a couple of bloopers—but I was on my way and that was all that mattered.

Don't get trapped into crazy schemes, either. I see guys getting down on one knee and swinging the bat with one hand. What good can that do? They should be in the batter's box swinging the bat with both hands and working on their timing or getting into a game and hitting the ball to the opposite field to get their confidence back. Every hitter who practices and works the right way will improve consistency, and that is what keeps away trouble.

Remember, hitting is not an exact science, but it isn't an unfathomable black art either. It's demanding, and it requires hitters to concentrate their physical—and their mental—efforts in mastering its many skills.

XII. The Game Before The Game

So now you've learned that baseball is as much a game of the mind as it is a game of physical skill. The *Baseball Register* and the *Baseball Almanac* are filled with the names of major leaguers who achieved success because they mastered the game as much with their mind as they did with their body.

You must do the same, regardless of your level of competition. The earlier you begin, the better your habits will become and the more you will be prepared for all situations. Remember, these are fundamental points, and you must master the fundamentals and begin good habits from the very beginning. They will stay with you forever, and in the end, your mastery of them may well determine just how successful you really will become. Let me review a few of these points.

Build a game plan every time you play. Know who is pitching and know what his strengths and weaknesses are. Know particularly what he likes to do to you—all the while recognizing your strengths and weaknesses and how you anticipate he'll come after you.

Then begin to build a game plan. The easiest way is by constructing certain situations which are based on what you know about the pitcher and what you know about yourself.

For example, pretend the count is 2-2. Do you think you will get a fastball because he is a good fastball pitcher? You know, too, that if you get the fastball, you'll be ready, because at 2-2 you must protect the plate, so you will go after anything close to the strike zone.

But now you have to cycle in the possibility that you may see a slider. Picture the pitch coming from his hand and how it will look as it heads toward the plate. Now, in the back of your mind, you are also prepared should he come with a slider or any other breaking pitch. Mentally prepare for them all by visualizing what his pitches look like and where they are apt to go. In that way, there will be no surprises because you at least have given yourself a preview of coming attractions.

Guess on pitches. About ninety-five percent of major league hitters say they never guess on pitches. "I anticipated what he was going to throw," is the popular line.

Let me tell you, there isn't much difference between guessing and anticipating if you have done your homework. All you need is to get some idea of how the pitcher will work on you and what you can do to cope with it, and then you have some way of "anticipating" what may happen. It is when you don't prepare yourself mentally that you get into the "guessing" routine, and that can be dangerous ground because you may not guess correctly.

So prepare, plan, and anticipate. Anything that you can bring to the plate will reduce the chance of sudden surprise. Put all of the surprises on your side, especially some unpleasant ones for the pitcher who will wind up muttering, "How did he know I was going to throw that pitch?"

Most importantly, you should practice. That word is probably used as much in this book as the phrase "opposite field," because I am such a staunch believer in both. But in this instance, I want to remind you to practice simulated situations that you could face in a game.

If the score is tied and there are two out and a man on second late in the game, what is your game plan as a hitter? And against this pitcher? What will *his* game plan most likely be? Get an idea of what might happen and what you wish to happen.

Use batting practice for this mental drill. Set up an imaginary situation with a man on first base and pretend the count is 1-2 in the pitcher's favor. Now, have the batting practice pitcher throw you a breaking ball, because in that situation you will most likely get that pitch. Now you will be familiar and have a good idea of just what the ball will do and how you can handle it if it is near the strike zone.

If nothing else, you will get good practice coping with breaking balls, and young hitters, particularly, can never get enough hitting practice against them. Keep coming up with all kinds of possible situations; we do that every day in spring practice for nearly an hour, and if it is important enough for big league players, then it certainly is a necessity for young players.

Although this doesn't apply to this book, don't fail to do this as a fielder, either. Go over every conceivable situation that could happen at your position, and check each of them off in your mind so the right response will click in at the appropriate time.

As much as getting you prepared to handle these situations, this drill also begins to create good habits, which, as I noted at the beginning of this chapter, are a must for young players. Make them a part of your routine for as long as you play the game—and such habits are useful away from the game, too, because they get you thinking and planning how you will handle problems that can arise later in your life away from the ball field.

I know that young players get bored with repetition, but I cannot stress too much just how important it is to practice game-situation plays time after time until they are mastered. It is the only way a player—and a team—can become better, and that goes for new players as well as older players. There is no such thing as "knowing it all."

Hitters, particularly, should never be satisfied. When they get a hit, they should be thinking about how they can get another . . . and another. There simply are not enough hits for any batter. Go and get them all.

Appendix

Youth Sports: Benefits and Responsibilities for the Athlete and Coach

Benefits of Participating in Sports

Sports for children have become so popular that an estimated 20 million American children between the ages of six and sixteen play one or more sports each year. This tremendous interest suggests that parents and children believe that competitive athletics contribute positively to children's development. Such a wholesale endorsement may be misleading, however, unless it is counterbalanced by the sobering statistic that approximately 70 percent of the children drop out of organized sports programs by age fifteen. Many of the children who drop out are the ones who could benefit most from organized sports if directed by competent coaches. Thus, every coach, parent and athlete should answer the questions, "What are the benefits of competitive sports for children?" and "How can I be sure that these benefits are available to all children who participate in youth sports?"

Clearly, sports can have both positive and negative effects on children, but positive results can occur only if coaches and athletes conduct themselves in responsible ways. Although many of the benefits are immediately detectable and of a short-term nature, the most sought-after and important contributions of sports to total development are those that last far beyond the athlete's playing days.

In order for the benefits of sports to be available for all children, they must be identified, valued and included in their practices and games. Following are some of the benefits that are most commonly associated with children's sports participation:

- developing various sports skills
- learning how to cooperate and compete

- developing a sense of achievement, which leads to a positive self image
- developing an interest in and a desire to continue participation in sports during adulthood
- developing independence
- developing social skills
- learning to understand and express emotion, imagination, and appreciation for what the body can do
- developing speed, strength, endurance, coordination, flexibility, and agility
- developing leadership skills
- learning to make decisions and accept responsibilities

The Role of the Coach in Youth Sports

The coach of young athletes is the single most important adult in all of children's athletics. Other adults, such as officials and administrators, have important responsibilities, too, but no task is as important as that of the coach, who must guide young children physically, socially and emotionally as they grow from childhood through adolescence into adulthood.

The youth sports coach is required to play many roles. Most prominent among these are being a teacher and an instructor of skills, a friend who listens and offers advice, a substitute parent when the athlete's mother or father is not available or accessible, a medical advisor who knows when and when not to administer first aid and emergency care, a disciplinarian who rewards and corrects behavior, and a cheerleader who provides encouragement when everything goes wrong.

The age and development level of the athletes will determine how frequently the coach is asked to assume the various roles. Indeed, coaches may find themselves switching roles minute by minute as the fast-moving, complex nature of a contest calls for different responsibilities. The coach's responsibilities in each of the most common roles are discussed in the following sections.

The Coach As a Teacher

Although all of the coach's responsibilities are important, none is more important than being a good teacher. No matter how adept a coach is in other roles, these successes cannot overcome the harm caused by bad teaching. What then, are the characteristics of a good teacher?

Good teachers know what they are attempting to teach and are able to **select appropriate content** for the various levels of ability of their team members. Good teachers are **well organized,** both for the long-term season and in their daily practice and game plans. Good teacher are also **interested in the progress** of all their team members, including those who are inept and slow-learning. In summary, good teachers must love their athletes and their sport so much that practice sessions and games are joyful experiences for coaches and athletes.

The Coach As a Friend

Children play sports for many reasons, but one of the most frequently cited is that they like to be with friends and make new friends. Often, the most important role of the coach is just being a friend to a child who has none.

Being a friend to a friendless child often requires initiative and extra work for a coach, because such children are often unskilled and may have personality characteristics which make it difficult for other children to like them. Often the attention and affection by a coach is a sufficient stimulus for other team members to become more accepting, too. Regardless of the effort required, the coach must ensure that every child feels accepted as a member of the team.

The coach as a friend must be enthusiastic about sports and the participation of all children. Good friends are motivators who reward players with compliments and positive instruction instead of concentrating on errors. Good friends make children feel good about playing sports.

The Coach As a Substitute Parent

Nearly 50 percent of today's young athletes are likely to live in single-parent families. Whether or not coaches want the role of being a substitute parent, they are likely to acquire it. Even those children who live with both parents are apt to need the advice of their coach occasionally.

One of the most useful functions of the coach as a substitute parent is simply to listen to the child's problems. Frequently, the mere presence of an adult listener who inserts an occasional question to assist the child in clarifying the problem is all that is needed. As a coach, you must be careful not to judge the appropriateness of a parent's actions. In most instances the problems between parents and children are simply misunderstandings about children's desires and responsibilities. Such misunderstandings can usually be resolved by discussion, persuasion and compromise. However, in situations where parental actions are resulting in physical or mental abuse, the coach should contact professional counselors who are equipped to deal with such problems.

The Coach As Medical Advisor

Medical problems should be left to medical personnel who are equipped to deal with them. However, as a coach you are usually the first person at the scene of a youth sports injury and, therefore, are obligated to provide or obtain the necessary first aid. In addition, your judgment is likely to be called upon in situations where an injury has occurred and a decision must be made about whether the athlete should return to practice or competition.

A prudent policy for you is to resist making decisions which others are more qualified to make. You should seek the advice of medical personnel when injuries occur. Encourage your athletes to report aches, pains and injuries that are likely to impede their performance. Despite the emphasis on short-term objectives, your job is to safeguard the health of the athletes so that they are able to participate fully in physical activity well beyond the childhood years.

The Coach As Disciplinarian

One of the most frequently cited values of youth sports is their alleged contribution to the behavior and moral development of athletes. However, there are instances in children's sports where coaches and athletes have behaved in socially unacceptable ways. Obviously, attitudes and behaviors can be affected both positively and negatively in sports.

The first step to being a good disciplinarian is to establish the rules that will govern the athletes' behavior. These rules are more likely to be accepted and followed if the athletes have a voice in identifying them. Secondly, you must administer the rules fairly to all athletes. Desirable behavior must be enforced and undesirable actions must be corrected.

The Coach As a Cheerleader

Young athletes are likely to make numerous mental and physical errors as they attempt to learn specific skills. For that reason, their coaches must be tolerant of mistakes and eager to applaud any actions that represent improvement in performance.

Young athletes respond well to praise that is earned and given sincerely. Conversely, they are not very tolerant of criticism, especially when it occurs in association with a coach's expectations that are beyond their capacities or abilities. You must know your athletes so well that your requests are likely to result in a high ratio of successes to failures. When you choose tasks that are challenging but are likely to be done successfully you are in a position to be a **positive coach.** Positive coaches are likely to have fewer discipline problems than coaches who expect too much and then focus on inappropriate behavior. Being a positive coach is a good way to build the self-esteem that all young athletes need in order to feel successful about their sports participation.

The Role of the Athlete

A successful youth sports experience places demands on athletes as well as coaches. These responsibilites should be stated so that athletes and their parents understand what is expected of them. Some of the most important responsibilities of athletes are as follows:

- treat all teammates and opponents with respect and dignity
- obey all team and league rules
- give undivided attention to instruction of techniques, skills and drills
- always practice and play with a clear mind
- report all injuries to the coach for further medical evaluation
- discourage rule violations by teammates or opponents
- play under emotional control at all times
- avoid aggressive acts of self-destruction
- compliment good performances of teammates and opponents
- return to play when an injury is completely rehabilitated

Summary

Youth sports are designed to provide benefits to both athletes and coaches. However, these benefits cannot be obtained in the absence of clearly defined responsibilities. When both coaches and athletes accept and carry out the responsibilities defined in this introduction, then the benefits of youth sports participation are likely to be realized.

Vern Seefeldt, Ph.D.
Director
Youth Sports Institute
Michigan State University

About The Authors

TONY OLIVA

Tony Oliva was one of the American League's outstanding hitters during his career with the Minnesota Twins, from 1964 thru 1976, and since then he has been recognized as one of baseball's outstanding hitting instructors, a fulltime role he has held with the Twins since 1986. Tony won back-to-back batting titles in both his rookie season (.323) and in his second season (.321), and he added a third AL crown in 1971 with a .337 average. He was selected American League Rookie of the Year in 1964, and that league's player of the year in 1965 as he helped the Twins to the American League pennant. Tony also tied Hall of Famer Joe DiMaggio's record of being named to the league All-Star team during his first six seasons. In 1973, he hit the first home run by a designated hitter and a year later, led the majors in pinch hitting with a .538 mark. He finished his career with a lifetime .304 average, making him a Hall-of-Fame candidate, and has worked for the Twins organization as a minor league manager as well as in various coaching positions.

JACK CLARY

Freelance writer Jack Clary has co-authored, written and edited more than two dozen books on a variety of sports subjects during some 30 years as a journalist. These include a trivia book on the Minnesota Twins, and another, *So You Think You're a Baseball Fan* He also authored books with NFL Hall of Famers Paul Brown (*PB*); Andy Robustelli (*Once a Giant, Always ...*) as well as with former Orioles pitcher and television broadcaster Jim Palmer (*Jim Palmer's Way to Fitness*); former Bengals quarterback Ken Anderson (*The Art of Quarterbacking*). Some other books include *Great Moments in Pro Football, Careers in Sports, Army vs. Navy* and *The Game-makers* with such renowned coaches as Tom Landry, John Madden, Chuck Noll, Don Shula and others. In addition to working as a consultant in all aspects of sports communications and marketing for his firm, Sports Media Enterprise, Clary spent 17 years as a sportswriter and columnist for The Associated Press, New York World Telegram & Sun and the Boston Herald Traveler.

Credits
Book Production/Design: Mountain Lion, Inc.
Cover Design: Michael Bruner
Copyediting: Deborah Crisfield
Photographs: Michael Plunkett
Typesetting: Elizabeth Typesetting Company
Mechanical: Production Graphics
Cover Photograph © Michael Zagaris

KIRBY PUCKETT

Kirby Puckett, in just five seasons as a major league player, already walks with an elite group of players, He is the fourth player ever to get 1,000 hits in his first five seasons. His .356 average in 1987 was the highest by an American League right-handed hitter since Hall of Famer Joe DiMaggio hit .357 in 1941; and since World War II only Stan Musial, Hank Aaron, a pair of Hall of Famers, and Don Mattingly have matched Puckett's .350 average, 200 hits, 40 doubles, 20 homers and 100 RBI and runs scored in a single season. He has a .320 lifetime average and has been acclaimed as one of the AL's best fielding centerfielders. In addition to three All-Star Game appearances, he also batted .357 in helping the Twins to the World Championship in 1986.